FREE THE
MANCHESTER UNITED
ONE

FREE THE MANCHESTER UNITED ONE

The Inside Story of Football's Greatest Scam

GRAHAM SHARPE

 ROBSON BOOKS

First published in Great Britain in 2003 by Robson Books,
The Chrysalis Building, Bramley Road, London W10 6SP

A member of Chrysalis Books Group plc

British Library Cataloguing in Publication Data
A catalogue record for this title is available from the
British Library.

ISBN 1 86105 633 8

Typeset by FiSH Books, London WC1
Printed by Creative Print & Design (Wales), Ebbw Vale

Contents

Manchester United Museum and Tour Centre displays one of the most comprehensive collections of football memorabilia in Britain. It is open seven days a week from 9.30 a.m. until 5.00 p.m. Tours of the stadium are also available. Admission charges apply and times of tours and entry to the Museum are subject to alteration.

Manchester United Museum
Sir Matt Busby Way
Old Trafford
Manchester
M16 0RA
Tel: +44(0) 161 868 8635
Fax: +44(0) 161 868 8862
Email: mark.wylie@manutd.co.uk
Website: www.manutd.com

To Layne and Lizzie Patterson,
the most hospitable Manchester United
fans in the land.

Preamble

Out for my morning run, I spotted a football sitting forlornly several yards inside the wire surrounding the pitch on which I had played most of my Sunday football career. I wondered whether I should rescue the sorry-looking ball and take it home for my sons to use as a kickabout. Was it worth the effort and slight risk involved in shinning over the fence to rehabilitate the football? I couldn't tell from where I was whether the ball was usable or a deflated reject. There was only one way to find out. I climbed over the fence and picked up the ball. It was soft, needed inflating, but felt as though it would respond to a pump. Getting back over the fence with its jagged, wiry strands was not easy, but I managed it. The football did service as a training ball and the boys and their team were all well pleased that I'd bothered to take the trouble to rescue it and allow it to resume a useful existence.

Foreword

I first came across the story of the 'bent' match between Manchester United and Liverpool while researching my book on the history of betting in football, *Gambling On Goals*. I was intrigued by the bare bones of the tale, the best-documented example of a genuinely 'squared' game among so many rumoured fixes and riggings that can never be conclusively proved. The most fascinating aspect of the game was the insistence of one of the so-called ring-leaders that he was innocent. Of the eight players subsequently barred *sine die*, he was the only one whose suspension was maintained until he was far too old to make a comeback.

Six of the guilty parties admitted their involvement and were pardoned. One tragically died in the First World War. But Enoch 'Knocker' West went to his grave still adamantly declaring he had been wronged. I thought it would be a fascinating exercise to find out how and why the whole incident had come about. But I also wanted to establish whether there was the slightest chance that Enoch had indeed been wrongly accused and, if so, to win for him a posthumous pardon or, at least, an acknowledgement from the football authorities that he had been hard done by. This is the story of that match and my efforts to 'Free the Manchester United One'.

Acknowledgements

Trying to re-create a time nearly a century removed from one's own is not possible without a great deal of help and I must place on record my gratitude to those who selflessly assisted my endeavours. Among them I include Simon Inglis, whom I had admired from afar, and whose own *Soccer In The Dock* had encouraged my initial interest in this game. Simon kindly permitted me to borrow his original notes, compiled when writing about the match in that book. We enjoyed an Italian meal together, during the course of which it emerged that we share a love of pretty obscure mid-sixties psychedelia and blues music – me only listening, but Simon often playing.

Simon remains convinced that his book *Sightlines* (Yellow Jersey, 2000) was badly treated by the judges of the prestigious William Hill Sports Book of the Year, which award I initiated. I know he is wrong but understand why he feels unable to attend the ceremonies at which the annual winner is announced. The invitation is there permanently.

Chas Sumner, Chester City archivist, helped me to locate details of the mysterious Lol Cook, who was one of the eight players suspended but who was listed as being a Chester player and whose relationship with the United and Liverpool players was initially unclear.

My good friend and former colleague on the board of Wealdstone FC, Layne Paterson – who has been nurturing his own Manchester United-related book idea for more years than I care to recall – hunted through his massive collection of United books to track down references to the match and those who took part in it. I'm not sure that he didn't welcome the excuse to pore over the volumes without attracting the criticism of his lovely wife Lizzie. I am delighted to dedicate this book to the two of them.

David Barber, Librarian and Archivist at the FA, allowed me access to his volumes and, although we were unable to locate the minutes of the Commission that investigated the match, I found some helpful material there. Hugh Hornby at the National Football Museum; Banker and Liverpool enthusiast Alan Hindley supplied me with stats and details; while Knocker's grandson, Roger West, was enthusiastic and helpful in progressing the project.

My family – Sheila, Steeven and Paul – suffered, as ever, when, from being the leader of the anti-Man U brigade, I became obsessed with the club's history, up to and including 1915, for the duration of the book.

I found much useful material at the British Newspaper Library in Colindale – even though they occasionally seemed unwilling to let me in. Can't blame them really.

It was great to find Knocker's son, Eric, so vibrantly alive, if still somewhat unsure about his feelings towards his father – perhaps this book will help him in that respect. After writing the book, I have a grudging respect and affection for someone who was clearly a difficult character to deal with, who insisted on ploughing his own furrow and who didn't suffer fools gladly, if at all – perhaps I recognised many of my own traits in there. Well done, Knocker, guilty or innocent!

Thanks very much to everyone else who helped out.

Graham Sharpe,
August 2003

Prologue – The Pre-fix

Monday-night regulars hunched over their pints at The Dog and Partridge pub in Manchester had been digesting the latest news of the war, and now their discussion turned to the forthcoming big game between Manchester United and Liverpool to be held a week later – on Good Friday 1915. There was little optimism in the air. It was a 'must-win' match for the relegation-threatened Old Trafford club against rivals who had a cushion of a few points but who were not wholly out of the woods.

As the drinkers pondered how United boss John Robson would plot a course to safety in the final eight games of the season, some of them might have noticed a little knot of men sitting in the corner, deep in animated conversation. Keen Manchester United supporters and knowledgeable followers of football and cricket would have remarked that the small group contained some familiar faces.

Wasn't that United centre half Arthur Whalley who had just gone up to the bar to order a round of pints? And the chap who'd just called out to him to 'hurry up' – didn't he resemble prolific forward Enoch 'Knocker' West? Surely one of the other fellows was West's great pal and inside forward partner Sandy Turnbull? As for that other bloke with them – wasn't he Jackie Sheldon, who'd been a winger with United until he'd left to play for Liverpool, just before Christmas 1913? Could that be Lancashire cricketer Lol Cook with them?

Most of them were likely to be in one of the two teams lining up the following Friday. But then, why shouldn't they get together for a friendly glass or two before the game? Mind you, it didn't seem that friendly. They weren't getting on at all well. A few heated words had been exchanged. Voices were raised. Other patrons stopped

talking and strained to hear what the argument was about. Some
bold souls were about to go and ask the group for their opinion
about the forthcoming match and to seek reassurance that United
would survive. But the footballers – if indeed that was who they
were – quickly finished their drinks and departed into the typically
damp, late-March Mancunian twilight.

Three days later, on the eve of the vital match – April Fool's day,
as fate would have it – at another pub, just around the corner from
the Great Central Station in Manchester, a small gathering was once
again drawing itself to the attention of locals enjoying an evening
pint. Sheldon and West were identified, along with Manchester
United forward George Anderson and a couple of other men.
Snippets of the conversation between them were overheard and later
repeated around the city. Rumours began to fly through this close-
knit community of footballing men, many of whom immediately
made a beeline for their bookies...

1

The Birth of Match Fixing

Considering the number of football matches that have been played in Britain since the game became organised into leagues and subject to strict rules, the percentage that has been proved to have been manipulated, rigged or fixed, is tiny. Naturally, the cases that have come to light have been highly sensationalised in the newspapers and topped with lurid banner headlines. Although betting has proved to be the motive behind some games that were rigged to produce pre-determined results, it has not been the only incentive. In the days of maximum wages – a restrictive practice that was finally ended in 1961 – many players who had been tempted by offers of additional payments 'under the counter' would agree to help 'throw' games in order to influence promotion or relegation issues that might have had drastic financial implications for the clubs involved. In his excellent book, *Soccer in the Dock*, Simon Inglis points out:

> In the decade or so before 1914 the football authorities had to deal with a whole catalogue of misdemeanours, almost all of them related to financial irregularities. More serious was the matter of rigging match results. There were two leading motives behind attempts to 'fix' matches. The first and most common reason...was in order to achieve a certain League placing. These rigged games always took place near the end of the season and perhaps helped guarantee promotion or a 'talent money' placing, or maybe helped a club avoid relegation. The second reason for rigging a result was in order to gain financially from betting.

Another early example of dodgy deeds on the football field was recorded in March 1878 by the *Darwen News*. In a report of a match between Darwen and local rivals Turton it was alleged that the latter's 'goalkeeper did pretty well, but we should recommend him to cease his contention with the spectators and keep his money in his pocket.' In 1890 a more blatant type of attempted match 'fixing' was seen at Shieldfield in Scotland where teams arriving to play local side Royal Oak were warned that any goalkeeper foolish enough to attempt to prevent their star centre forward from scoring, or saving his shots, was liable to have the utmost difficulty in departing from the ground with limbs intact!

In May 1900 Jack Hillman, Burnley's goalkeeper, was suspended for a year by a joint Football League and Football Association Commission after trying to bribe Nottingham Forest players to lose a game that would otherwise doom Burnley to relegation. Forest players rejected the Burnley offer of £2 per head to 'take it easy'. And even after the inducement was increased to £4 – when Burnley were 2–0 down at half time – the bribe produced the same negative reaction. Forest eventually won 4–0. A more bizarre reason for trying to fix a result emerged in 1911 when Middlesbrough boss Andy Walker was banned for trying to predetermine the outcome of a game against bitter local rivals Sunderland – a game that 'Boro' won 1–0. Allegedly, the match was fixed in order to assist the political aspirations of Middlesbrough Chairman Lieutenant-Colonel Gibson Poole, who was standing in the forthcoming General Election. Following the scandal, Poole was banned from football for life and also failed to win the seat. However, the scandal did not prevent him from eventually receiving a knighthood – on New Year's Day 1935.

In 1912 Richard McNeall was jailed for two months after admitting writing to Burnley FC and Norwich City, purporting to be the goalkeeper of teams they were about to play, and offering to throw the games for £20. Even Inspector Clouseau might reasonably have been expected to have cracked that particular case.

Having researched many so-called betting-related match-fixing scandals I have come across a great many references of this nature. It is impossible to deny that match-rigging has taken place, but perfectly possible to argue that betting as the main cause has often been over-played. The earliest reference to betting on a football match I have discovered refers to the first FA Cup Final ever played – on 16 March 1872 – in which the 4–7 favourites The Royal Engineers became the sport's first beaten odds-on hot shots. The ironically named Betts scored the only goal of the game for the outsiders, The Wanderers. However, there was no suggestion of match-fixing in this case.

It was not until 1892, exactly twenty years later, that officials and players were banned from betting on matches. And in 1902 the FA attempted the impossible – trying to ban everyone who attended a football match from betting on its outcome. The authorities now saw a new 'menace' on the horizon – betting coupons. In 1909 three men caught distributing football betting coupons outside Villa Park on a match day were arrested and offered a choice of a £1 fine or fourteen days in jail. In 1910 legendary goalkeeper Billy 'Fatty' Foulke, of Sheffield United and England, was prosecuted for permitting his retirement pub – the Duke Inn in Sheffield – to be used for the purposes of betting.

The football authorities were definitely feeling uneasy about the potential influence of betting on the game. In 1910 J C Clegg, a senior FA official, was warning, 'If ever betting got a firm foothold, the game as we know it would be done forever.' A 1938 publication, *The Story of the Football League*, referring to the 1911–12 season, revealed:

At this time the game began to be the object of increased activity among betting agents who did not hesitate to get into contact with players and give rise to suspicions regarding the bona-fides of certain games, and this brought a declaration from the Committee that any participation in betting on the games by any official or player would be dealt with as misconduct and be severely visited.

In September 1912 the Football League Management Committee warned against 'a number of betting agents, who are sending circulars and coupons' to players and officials. Coupon betting was causing such concern to the authorities that in 1913 the FA set up a commission to investigate the problem. Players' Union representatives, officials and directors all took part in the investigation. The FA's Commission reported that betting on the game was 'prevalent throughout the country' and, despite finding no serious evidence of match-rigging related to gambling, recommended permanent suspension for anyone in the game found guilty of any involvement with betting. In addition to calling for a life ban for any official, referee, linesman or player proved to have taken part in coupon betting, the Commission recommended that 'clubs be required to insert a clause in their agreements with players providing that the agreement be terminated upon it being proved that a Player has taken part in coupon football betting.' In February 1913 the FA Management Committee approved the resolution, 'This Committee regrets to learn that coupon betting and press competitions in the nature of coupons are being extensively used, to the serious detriment of the game. The Committee seriously warns all players and officials that they are determined to do all in their power to suppress the evil and will not hesitate to take extreme measures to that end.'

In March 1913 the *Morning Post* estimated that two million football coupons were being circulated nationally on a weekly basis. Writing in the *Spectator*, Charles E B Russell was blaming betting for unrest at games, and hinting at skulduggery. He suggested:

When once the canker of ulterior gain as the result of a win enters the game, part of the genuine healthy pleasure goes. Sometimes the violent scenes which have taken place upon football fields may be traced to large numbers of spectators having lost money owing to the favourite team not having won, and to there being a general suspicion that the goalkeeper or some other member of the losing side has sold the match.

Speculation, rather than evidence, I think, and almost a charge that spectators might be looking to influence the outcome for betting purposes via crowd violence. By July 1913 the issue had reached the House of Commons where politicians debated the Ready Money Football Betting Bill. The Right Honourable W Hayes Fisher told Members of Parliament, 'The FA has long been determined to endeavour to free this game from the excrescences which have grown upon it in connection with betting and gambling.' In November 1913 the FA's Management Committee declared itself to be 'anxious to eliminate all species of speculation as being detrimental to the best interests of the game, the players and officials, and hope for the very healthy co-operation of all clubs and officials to maintain the purity of the sport'.

In 1914 a bookmaker's father was imprisoned for five months after being found guilty of offering £55 to a player to influence the outcome of a match. The convicted man was named as Pascoe Bioletti. His son, William Alfred Bioletti, of Hove, in Sussex, operated a football coupon betting business based in Geneva. The player approached was, bizarrely enough, the totally incorruptible England and West Bromwich Albion skipper Jesse Pennington – as highly regarded in his day as Bobby Charlton, Gary Lineker and Alan Shearer have been by later generations. The cash on offer was £5 per player to ensure that Albion did not win their imminent game at home to Everton on 29 November 1913. The incident was reported to the police who organised a 'sting' operation. The game went ahead and ended in a draw. Afterwards Pennington approached the man and asked for his 'bung'. At this point the law appeared and the culprit was taken into custody. It was later alleged that Bioletti had also endeavoured to 'nobble' Birmingham captain Francis Womack.

These bungled efforts to fix games do not give the overwhelming impression that there was a well-organised and ruthless syndicate in the background. Rather they seem like the efforts of a few individuals who had made naïve and hopelessly ill-targeted attempts to influence a couple of games. The plots had been rumbled almost immediately and promptly and properly dealt with. Football and social historian Nicholas Fishwick captured the essence of the dilemma facing the game's administrators when he wrote in his *English Football and Society 1910–50*:

> The football authorities were hostile to betting on football, they claimed, because it damaged the sport's reputation and threatened the fairness of the game. This involved taking every possible step to prevent betting from influencing football, while strenuously denying that any such influence existed.

In a March 1914 article, not in itself notably friendly towards the concept of football betting, the *Glasgow Herald* (without apparent sarcasm or irony) declared, 'There is no suggestion that the professional football player is mixed up in any dishonourable way with coupon betting. His sense of fair play is beyond question. But he may, and frequently does, "put a little bit on" coupons.' The *Herald* also estimated that 'one bookmaker distributes a weekly average of about 40,000 coupons in Glasgow and district' which gives some idea of the appeal and popularity of football-related betting at the time. *Athletic News* considered 'The Integrity of Games' in a December 1915 article which commented:

In days past there have been a few games in which suspicions have been roused. Perhaps there was ground for complaint over some contests in which a club has dwelt in the safety zone and their opponents have been in fear of relegation. There have, however, been many explanations for most of these games, such as the indifference and the predilections of one set of players, and the earnestness and the fierceness of those who were striving to avoid a lower division of football. Matches of an unsatisfactory character have become increasingly rare.

If this Manchester United–Liverpool match has been proved to be a fake, it must not be wildly assumed that footballers as a class are a pack of scoundrels. We should not forget how Charles Thomson of Sunderland, Pennington of West Bromwich and Womack of Birmingham acted when they were offered bribes by men who had interests outside football. It would be just as logical to infer from these cases that all players were sufficiently honest as to deduce that all players are rogues from this Manchester United–Liverpool fiasco. The integrity of League football as a whole is as beyond impunity.

But even today, football has an ambiguous attitude to gambling. Players are still barred from betting on matches, yet the game benefits financially from gambling through the football pools and by permitting clubs to have betting shop facilities in their grounds.

2

Setting the Scene

Before the kick-off time of matches played on Friday 2 April 1915, the English Football League Division One table looked like this:

Team	Played	Won	Drawn	Lost	For–Against	Points
Oldham	31	15	9	7	64–48	39
Manchester City	32	14	11	7	44–32	39
Blackburn Rovers	33	16	7	10	72–52	39
Sheffield Weds.	33	13	12	8	56–48	38
Everton	32	15	7	10	66–42	37
Sunderland	32	17	3	12	73–62	37
Sheffield United	31	12	11	8	40–32	35
West Brom. Albion	32	12	10	10	39–31	34
Bradford City	32	11	12	9	50–41	34
Bradford	31	14	6	11	52–55	34
Middlesbrough	33	11	10	12	53–66	32
Burnley	31	13	5	13	50–42	31
Aston Villa	31	11	8	12	49–62	30
Liverpool	33	10	9	14	54–67	29
Bolton Wanderers	33	10	6	17	63–78	26
Tottenham Hotspur	33	7	11	15	49–73	25
Newcastle	31	8	9	14	38–42	25
Manchester United	31	7	11	13	39–48	25
Notts County	33	7	11	15	36–53	25
Chelsea	30	6	12	12	38–49	24

Manchester United (who had only gloried in that title since April 1902, when they had changed their name from Newton Heath) had been First Division champions as recently as the 1910–11 season. But when Liverpool came to Old Trafford on Good Friday 2 April 1915 United were languishing third from the bottom of the First Division, having only gained 25 points from 31 games. Liverpool themselves – despite frequently repeated claims that they were now free of relegation worries – were, in fact, far from safe. They had only picked up 29 points from 33 games, putting them in fourteenth position out of the twenty teams in the table. Top of the table were Oldham, with 39 points from 31 games. Then came Manchester City, with 39 points from 32 games, and Blackburn Rovers, with 39 from 33. Chelsea were bottom, with 24 points from 30 games.

This was an extremely tight division in which one might think every point was vital – especially as it should be remembered that a win only earned two points in those days. Today, the rivalry between Manchester United and Liverpool is fierce, and the thought that either side might do the other a favour – even for pecuniary reward – is impossible to contemplate. In those days, though, as United chronicler Richard Kurt points out, 'The now infamous rivalry was not yet of sufficient power to make this a game they – Liverpool – HAD to win.'

The fact that Britain was now eight months into what would become known as the First World War – or the 'Great War' – posed an added problem for Football League players and officials alike. The war broke out on 4 August 1914. At the beginning there had been no conscription and although many football players had left their clubs to volunteer for the forces, it was decided by both the Football League and the Football Association that the full season's fixture list should be completed. That league games were continuing to be played, despite the mounting death toll in France, was causing rumblings of discontent among military leaders and politicians. But this was not a universal view. Some people argued that sporting contests allowed civilians an opportunity to let off steam and provided much-needed relief and entertainment for those on leave from the front, or left at home while their loved ones went off to war, or unable, through being too unfit, too young

or too old, to sign on for the forces. Indeed some ever
were the FA to cancel all sporting contests for the u.
conflict it would be an admission of defeat and an indicatiu.
enemy that Britain was unable to maintain normal life in the tac
of the conflict.

However, at a special meeting of the Football League, held in
London a few days before the Good Friday match, Colonel C F
Grantham, commander of the 17th Battalion, the Duke of
Cambridge's Own Middlesex Regiment (Football), was hugely
critical of the level of recruitment from the sport. Colonel
Grantham, the top officer in the Footballers' Battalion, revealed that
only 122 professional players of an estimated 1,800 available had
joined up. He told those present, 'I am taking the opportunity to ask
you gentlemen if you and your clubs have done everything in your
power to point out to the men what their duty is.' Colonel Grantham
pulled no punches when he declared, 'It is no use mincing words. If
men who are fit and capable of doing so will not join, they and also
those who try by their words and actions to prevent them will have
to face the opinion of their fellow men publicly. I will no longer be
a party to shielding the want of patriotism of these men by allowing
the public to think they have joined the Football Battalion.'

Historian A F Pollard wrote to *The Times*, 'We view with
indignation and alarm the persistence of Association Football clubs
in doing their best for the enemy – every club that employs a
professional football player is bribing a much needed recruit to
refrain from enlistment and every spectator who pays his gate
money is contributing so much towards a German victory.' The
Dean of Lincoln wrote to the FA about 'onlookers who, while so
many of their fellow men are giving themselves in their country's
peril, still go gazing at football.' With such strong feelings being
aroused, there was a general belief that once the 1914–15 season
had been completed, league games were likely to be put on hold for
the duration of the war. This would have major financial
implications for the players.

Footballers at this time were most definitely not the well-paid and
over-pampered superstars of today. Among Football League players
there must have been an ominous feeling that if and when serious

football was resumed they may not be young enough, fit enough –
or perhaps alive enough! – to resume earning a living from the
game. The players must have been fearful for their futures – both
financial and physical. At that time players were the exploited
parties (the era of the multi-million pound soccer star was still to
come and would have seemed an unbelievable fantasy to them).
Attendances at matches could be huge, yet players' wages were
comparatively modest. Footballers were treated as little more than
talented slaves. The boardroom barons were the beneficiaries of the
players' skills – even though crowds were most certainly not
pouring into the grounds to watch well-to-do directors and
administrators in action.

If grievances over pay and conditions were widespread one might
have expected there to be an epidemic of crooked matches, as
players sought to earn themselves an illicit pay-day to tide them
over the probable hard times to come. Yet there is no reliable
evidence that any such outbreak of skulduggery occurred. Perhaps
circumstances had never previously been right for such a daring
operation to be planned and implemented.

What is beyond reasonable doubt, however, is that a number of
players plotted to ensure that Manchester United would win the
Good Friday match against Liverpool by a scoreline of 2–0, thereby
landing a betting coup by wagering on that pre-ordained scoreline at
odds of up to 8–1.

Betting on matches in this way was a comparatively new
phenomenon and it is unlikely that many bookmakers were prepared
to accept hefty bets based on correctly predicting the scores of
games. Their suspicions would already have been aroused by the
gossip in and around the game regarding the outcome of a small
number of the matches played in recent seasons.

Any players planning to make money on a rigged match would
have had to place their bets via trusted contacts, spreading the
wagers around different bookies to avoid suspicions being voiced
even before the match was played. They clearly couldn't have
placed the bets in their own names – even the most naïve of
bookmakers would have experienced a slight feeling of unease had
such a tactic been adopted. In fact 'layers' – those taking the bet –

would most certainly have refused to accept all but the very smallest stakes from such a source, and word would soon have spread along the grapevine that something dodgy was going on. Perhaps it did. Eamon Dunphy, in his book, *A Strange Kind of Glory*, says, 'For days before the match, rumours had circulated in Manchester that the result was "squared".' Another complication was that, at this time, team selection involved discussions by a number of people, rather than today's accepted practice of just one person – usually the manager or coach – making the decision. So it must have been difficult for the plotters-to-be who met up in the two pubs in the days before the big game to be sure their co-conspirators would actually be in the line up for the match.

Prior to this game, there had been two other Liverpool matches that had raised some concern. The first, a match against Newcastle in 1911, had been a draw. The second against Chelsea in March 1913 had ended in a 2–1 win for the Londoners. At the time, Liverpool had been in mid position in the First Division table and Chelsea were third from bottom. Afterwards, Arsenal Chairman Henry Norris (who, ironically, was suspended by the FA in 1927 for 'financial irregularities') wrote in a newspaper article that, 'had the Liverpool team as a whole desired to win the match they could have done so quite readily'. He expressed sorrow for 'the genuine triers in the Liverpool team'. It may or may not have been coincidental that Arsenal (then known as Woolwich Arsenal) were bottom of the table at the time. There seems to have been no suggestion that betting had played a part in deciding the outcome of that match. The poor performance was attributed to Liverpool's fixture list of three games in four days. Inquiries were held into both the Newcastle and Chelsea matches but nothing untoward was discovered in either case and the players were exonerated.

April Fool jokes were few and far between in the four-page edition of the racing and sporting paper the *Sporting Chronicle*, published on 1 April 1915 and costing one penny. The front page concerned itself mainly with horse and greyhound racing, and with running – or 'pedestrianism', as it was then known. The *Chronicle* reported that, 'A great foot race' was to be run at Westwood Grounds, Wigan on Saturday next 'between W Williamson and

J Brooks, who will run 100 yards for £30'. On Saturday 10 April at Salford Football Ground would take place the 'world's 220 yards championship between Jack Donaldson and W R Applegarth' for £200. Also on the front page there was news of rabbit coursing, pigeon flying and pigeon shooting.

The Good Friday football fixtures appeared on page two: FA League Division One – Aston Villa v Blackburn Rovers; Bolton Wanderers v Bradford; Chelsea v Bradford City; Everton v Burnley; Manchester United v Liverpool; Norwich City v Sheffield United; Spurs v Newcastle; Sunderland v Middlesbrough. (Had I been around in those days I would have been off to Hertfordshire, where Watford were entertaining my team, Luton Town, in a local Southern League derby, won, might I mention, 2–4 by the visitors.) The back page was where to find the football previews, under the heading 'Football Gossip':

> Except that Lacey displaces Fairfoul at right half back, the Liverpool team against Manchester United at Old Trafford tomorrow will be identical with that which drew with Newcastle last Monday. The position of Manchester United is now a desperate one and it will need success in their three Easter engagements against Liverpool, Newcastle and Bradford to take them out of the danger zone. The directors at their weekly meeting in consultation with the manager, Mr Robson and the Hon Sec Mr Bentley, decided upon several changes in the side to entertain Liverpool tomorrow. James Hodge is reintroduced at right back, while Anderson comes in at centre forward and Norton at outside left... At least two other players will accompany this team to Newcastle and the eleven must not be considered as also selected for Saturday. After the match the players travel to Harrogate where they will remain over the weekend, going on to Bradford on Monday morning.

The *Sporting Chronicle* also reported on prices for the Cup Final, which was to be held at Old Trafford: centre stand five shillings [25p]; five thousand stand seats at two and sixpence [12½p];

admission to ground one shilling [5p]. Kick off 3.30 p.m. The *Chronicle* also carried an advert for the forthcoming edition of its sister paper, the *Sunday Chronicle*, which promised readers such delightful articles as 'How To Breed A Virile Race' by Sir James Barr MD; and 'Modern Europe's Great Paradox – The most Irreligious Nation in the World Fighting for a Religious Maniac', by Austin Harrison.

Fans arriving for the Manchester United–Liverpool game were charged sixpence [2¹/₂p] or one shilling [5p] to get in and for one penny could buy the official match programme, Volume Five, Number 19, which offered eight pages of reading. The front page largely consisted of advertisements for The New Palace, in Oxford Street, Manchester, where a payment of sixpence – or fifteen shillings [75p] for a box – would secure the opportunity to see for the first time in the town none other than London Revue Idol, Shirley Kellogg, creator of 'the famous Wedding Glide'. The lovely Shirley was supported not only by Con Conrad's Novelty Minstrels but also Alice Hollander and Ernest H Mills – what a line-up!

On the inside the programme offered the opinion, 'The Merseyites will fight hard enough this afternoon to lift themselves even clearer than they are from the danger zone.' Well, perhaps not. On page five readers were reminded that, 'We cannot all go to France this Easter but we can all see All French – the Entente Cordiale Revue at the Ardwick Empire, featuring the Midnight Pearl Scene'. Those planning to attend were alerted to 'look out for the girl in the muff'. Those not attracted by matters *Français* could consider instead a visit to the Manchester Hippodrome where they could witness Albert Hengler's 'great water comedy' entitled 'Very Soft'. On page six there was a timely warning, 'The continuance of the war may prevent the opening of the season next September. In the result of the military situation taking a turn unfavourable to the Allies, football will be out of the question.' Then came editorial information that would suggest many footballers must have been harbouring deep concerns about their earning capacity in the future:

Only players with existing agreements will receive summer wages. The others cannot receive pay between 1 May–2 August, the earliest date fixed for training. The maximum wage will be £3 per week for the terms of engagement only – that is 2 August–29 April inclusive, with an increase of ten shillings [50p] per week for each two seasons of continuous service. There are to be thirty-nine weeks in the next football season and the maximum amount receivable by any player will be £117 – the present maximum is including summer wages and the leading players who depend exclusively upon football for a living will thus have their incomes more than halved.

That must have gone down well in the dressing room.

Page seven featured an advertisement extolling the virtues of the Manchester Brewery Co's Ales and Stouts – 'a bottle of Manchester Brewery Milk Stout contains more nutriment than a glass of milk and being sterilised it is free from the dangers that accompany the consumption of Milk. Taken with a little cheese or a crust of bread a glass of MB Milk Stout forms an easily digested and highly nutritive meal.'

At the bottom of the page were details of the forthcoming Central League match at Old Trafford between United and Southport Central for which boys would be admitted for a mere penny (wot, no girls?) while adults would be asked to shell out three [1¼p] or six pence [2½p]. On the back page of the programme was an advert for Harrops Stores in Manchester's Piccadilly which was 'filled to overflowing with up-to-date, high class goods – furniture, carpets, linoleum, oilcloths'.

The team line-ups featured on page three, together with the note that, 'Any change in teams will be notified by a number on the board which will be sent round the enclosures'. The only inaccuracy in the predicted line ups was that Lacey was replaced by Fairfoul. The stage was now set for one of the most infamous plots in footballing history.

3

Going West

The town of Hucknall was to play a significant part in the Good Friday match-fixing scandal. The Commission members who would ultimately investigate the allegations took a keen interest in the rash of gambling that had broken out there just before the game. More importantly, however, it was the home town of the leading player in the drama. Hucknall is situated on the west bank of the Leen Valley, seven miles north-west of Nottingham. It was listed as 'Hochenale' in the *Domesday Book* of 1086. The Torkard (or Torcard) family were important nearby residents from the end of the twelfth century and so, from 1295 until 1915, their name was added to the town's to form 'Hucknall Torkard', only to disappear during the second year of the First World War when the town reverted to plain old 'Hucknall' again.

The town's main claim to fame is that Lord Byron was buried there in 1824 in the family vault at the Parish Church of Saint Mary Magdalene, a few miles from the ancestral home of Newstead Abbey. Alongside him is his daughter Ada, Countess of Lovelace. The town's second celebrity connection was the 6ft 2in, 18-st barefist boxer Ben Caunt, who was born in 1814 near Newstead railway station. In 1838 Caunt became British heavyweight champion when he beat the reigning title holder Bendigo William Thompson in a little tussle that took place over 76 rounds. Caunt was baptised in Hucknall Torkard and also died there, in 1861.

The third famous resident of the town was Enoch James 'Knocker' West, born on 31 March 1886 (or 1884 according to one

15

source), who would grow up to become a famous – later, infamous – footballer, playing for Manchester United at the peak of his career. Some record books suggest that Enoch's middle name was John – and perhaps that was what he used to tell people. However, when I delved back into the official records of the 1901 Census held, coincidentally, on Enoch's fifteenth birthday, I discovered that he was listed as 'Enoch Jas West'. Whether the 'Jas' was short for James (or Jasper, or Jason), or was a name in its own right, it is difficult to know. But there was another 'Jas' listed at 2 Brook Street, Hucknall Torkard – where Enoch was living on 31 March 1901 – his 63-year-old grandfather, a 'collier hewer', whose name is recorded as Jas Richards. Presumably this was Enoch's maternal grandfather, married to Mary Ann, aged 58, a dressmaker. Both were from Leicester.

Enoch lived with his grandparents, together with an elder brother, sixteen-year-old Albert, and eight-year-old sister Constance. (According to one of his sons, Eric, who I contacted while researching this book, Enoch came from a family of ten; what happened to the other siblings I never discovered). Enoch and Albert were both listed as working as 'colliery pony driver'. All three children were born in Hucknall Torkard, but there is no mention of the children's parents. Surely they could not both have left the family? One of them, possibly, but it would seem more likely that accident, disease, or other tragedy had deprived the children of both mother and father, leaving them orphaned and dependant on their grandparents. An upbringing of that nature, with its obvious problems, might well explain why throughout his life Enoch would be described in terms such as 'stubborn', 'aggressive' and 'single-minded'. Character traits like these would no doubt have made him unpopular. West never quite matched the physical dimensions of the town's earlier great local sportsman, Caunt, peaking at 5ft 8in and weighing in at a modest 12st 6lb.

Less than a decade later, another local footballer was to make it to Manchester United. In 1922, Harry Williams, also a forward, played five League games for United, scoring twice, but failed to make the same impact as his Hucknall predecessor. As a boy West showed a natural aptitude for sports but he became a collier – coal mining had begun there in 1861 and there were two collieries in the town – before his natural footballing talent brought him to the attention of Sheffield United at the tender age of just fifteen. He reportedly became the youngest player to sign professional forms for them or, so it was claimed, any other professional football club.

However, his short stay there proved undistinguished and he joined non-League Hucknall Constitutional (possibly 'on loan' from Sheffield United). He quickly became one of the stars of the team, knocking in goals on a regular basis – including one recorded by the *Hucknall Torkard Dispatch and Leen Valley Mercury* on 9 February 1905 against local rivals Jardines, 'West converted a penalty, the custodian partially staying the progress of the ball.' West was soon being noticed by clubs at a higher level and the *Dispatch* reported on 20 April 1905 that, 'Holmes has been captured by Notts Forest, who may ere long include West in their ranks.' And on 22 June of that year, the *Nottingham Evening Post* was informing readers that Forest had acquired E J West (Hucknall and Sheffield United) in their 'full list of players for next season'.

Joining Forest for a rumoured £5 fee to Sheffield United, West made his debut in a red shirt four games into the season, at home to Bury in a 3–2 win on 16 September. He opened his account on his third outing with the club, on 30 September, scoring the only goal of a home fixture against Preston. In his first season, West totalled fourteen goals from 35 appearances for Forest, linking up with Grenville Morris, the first player to hit one hundred goals for the club, and playing in all five possible forward positions while listed in either the number eight or nine position on the team sheet. However, despite these efforts, Forest finished in nineteenth place and were relegated.

In his second season, West played 33 games, helping his side win the 1906–7 Second Division Championship and ensure promotion to the First Division. The following year, West was the league's top goal scorer. Forest would have to wait ninety years before another of their players – Pierre van Hooijdonk repeated that feat. West's goals were scored in 35 appearances – four of them in one game against Sunderland, on 9 November 1907 – and included hat-tricks against Chelsea and Blackburn Rovers. Forest finished the 1907–8 season in ninth place. In his *1998 Official History of Nottingham Forest*, Philip Soar wrote:

> Enoch 'Knocker' West was among the most celebrated and notorious of all Nottingham Forest players of any era. In 1907–8 he scored 27 (some records say 28, others 26) of Nottingham Forest's 59 goals and was the League's leading scorer, the only occasion a Nottingham Forest player had ever led the goal-scoring lists for the whole League until 1998. [Soar noted that 'West also holds the record for the longest ever suspension from the game'.]

West's versatility is shown by the different positions he occupied on the field, as indicated in the various match programmes, where he is listed at numbers seven, eight, nine, ten and eleven! On 24 February 1908, the local newspaper reported:

> Great satisfaction is felt in Nottingham Forest circles. That Enoch J West, centre forward, has been selected to play for England against Scotland, for it is felt that his abilities entitle him to that honour. He is now in his third year with the club. His transfer was secured on a nominal basis from Sheffield United for on the few occasions he played with the (Sheffield United) reserves he did not make friends. He is a native of Hucknall and is 23, standing 5ft 7$\frac{1}{2}$in high and weighing 11st 10lb.

It is not quite clear whether the phrase 'did not make friends' is meant to be taken literally or refers to his performance on the field. It is likely that the less-than-approachable nature of West's personality was evident even at this relatively early stage of his career. On 20 July 1908, another local newspaper article eulogised Enoch:

> West, the Nottingham Forester, is the greatest pivot of the age as he is credited with 27 goals and yet he only played in the centre in 19 matches. It is only right that I should add that West appeared in many other matches and occupied all three inside positions in turn. It is really calculated to make me laugh when

I recall that I saw West playing Outside Left at the commencement of last season. I was then so rash as to point out to Nottingham Forest that he was a wasted force in that position and that he should certainly be an inside man, if not a centre. Perhaps the Football Committee resent being told what they ought to do. After allowing him to expend his energy as an Outside Left for some weeks, they had to realise the logic of facts and the practicability of criticism. They brought West inside and he was chosen for the English League against the Scottish League as Inside Left.

Evidence of his stubborn nature, which was to reveal itself time and again, is furnished by the anonymous author of the piece, who reveals, 'After being ill in bed for several days he was so badly advised as to play (against Scotland) and severely handicap himself for honours in the future. Nevertheless, Enoch West is a capable forward and he should be persevered with in the centre.'

On 21 April 1909 West and two colleagues, Hooper and Spouncer, all grabbed hat-tricks as Leicester Fosse were walloped 12–0. Rumours that the match had been rigged were quickly dispelled when the opposition admitted that a number of their players had been the worse for wear following a heavy session the night – or even nights – before. One of the Leicester players' former team-mates, R F Turner, had got married and the already doomed-to-relegation Fosse players had helped him celebrate enthusiastically. Nevertheless their keeper, A P Bailey, an England international, had to face an investigating committee when he was accused, but acquitted, of taking bribes. This was the penultimate game of a season in which Forest dropped to fourteenth place. West had played 34 League matches for 22 goals, this season appearing in just the number nine and eleven positions.

In the 1909–10 season, Forest again stagnated in fourteenth place, with West playing 31 League matches and notching seventeen goals. He was missing from the side for the last seven games of the season, presumably through injury – although he might have fallen out with the club hierarchy while trying to secure a better deal for himself.

On 9 November 1909 an event of great import took place in Enoch's life – he became a father for the first time, when his son Eric was born. Perhaps it was no coincidence that on 27 November, just a couple of weeks later, he produced his most significant display. Away to Manchester United, West and striking partner Morris both hit hat-tricks in a 2–6 victory in front of 12,000 fans. Remarkably, this result came in a season when United were playing well, eventually finishing in fifth place. Someone important in the upper echelons at Old Trafford clearly took note of West's performance.

West's last goal for Forest was in a 1–1 home draw against Arsenal on 2 March. It brought his final tally for the club to exactly one hundred League and Cup goals in 183 appearances. West's last appearance for the club – starting at number eleven for the only time that season – was in a goalless home draw against Preston on 25 March 1910. Knocker, at the time living at 110 Montague Road, Hucknall, signed for Manchester United in June 1910 for a reported £450 fee, after the *Daily Dispatch* reported on 20 June 1910:

Under the new scheme West, the Nottingham Forester, who has joined the ranks of Manchester United will probably have received a share of his transfer fee. He has been five seasons at Nottingham and in the ordinary course of events would have expected a benefit there next season. As he is only 26 he ought to be of great service to the Old Trafford club. Mr (Ernest) Mangnall is to be congratulated, I think, on making one of the two captures of the close season. The other was, of course, the transfer of 'Tim' Coleman from Everton to Sunderland.

Another media report of the deal, by local reporter 'Trentsider', noted:

The transfer of Enoch J West from Nottingham Forest to Manchester United, though not unexpected, caused some surprise in football circles in Nottingham. It had been common knowledge for a long time that West and the Forest committee were not in agreement. Indeed, previous negotiations for his transfer have taken place, but West stubbornly [that descriptive word again – GS] refused the terms submitted to him.

He had not been re-engaged by the Forest and it is understood that he was firm in his demand that he was, by right, entitled to a benefit next season. Under the new rules he has, so it is understood, received a fair amount on his transfer and it is certain that the United have had to offer him favourable terms to join them.

West is powerfully built and active and there can be no doubt that on his day he is a fine, bustling centre forward as he demonstrated to his 'new chums' at Clayton last season when, along with Grenville Morris, he performed the 'hat-trick' against them. He was disappointing at the end of that campaign and appeared to have lost some of his pace, but if he regains this he should render splendid service to the Mancunians who are to be congratulated on their capture.

West has been with Forest for five seasons and is now 26. Born at Hucknall, Torkard was first discovered by Sheffield United. After only a few trials he was allowed to go to a Lincolnshire club, where he attracted the notice of the Forest. They were able to obtain his transfer from Sheffield United for an 'old song' and he proved to them a very serviceable and versatile forward. West stands 5ft 7in [having apparently shrunk by half an inch! – GS] and weighs about 12st 7lb.

Enoch had evidently worked hard to bulk up physically during the previous couple of seasons, having put on 11lb while at Nottingham Forest. His former club's fortunes slumped after Enoch's departure, and in the 1913–14 season they finished bottom of the Second Division and had to seek re-election. Forest must have needed the money from the deal, because by early 1915 they were so hard up they had to advise the Football League that they could no longer honour their debts. Forest had to be propped up with a grant and a weekly payment to keep them afloat.

One stipulation of the move to Manchester United was that West should give up his cricketing interests – he was good enough to be on the ground staff for Lancashire County Cricket Club, at Old Trafford cricket ground. Intriguingly, Lol Cook, later his co-accused in the match-fixing scandal, was a top-class bowler for Lancashire.

West's grandson, Roger, told me that he understood that 'Knocker' had been a spin bowler at Lancashire but that the committee asked him to leave when they discovered he was also playing football for Manchester United. 'They believed that football was not a game for the kind of gentlemen who played cricket.' The Rev Malcolm Lorimer, Lancashire CCC statistician, believes that Enoch played for the County's second eleven and was 'possibly also a local professional in the Leagues.'

There is also a record of Enoch West playing for Manchester Cricket Club as a professional, if only in one match, in which he scored ten not out and bowled a short spell in which he picked up no wickets and conceded twelve runs. He is also listed in 1913 records, bowling twelve overs, taking six wickets for 57 runs with one maiden over. No batting statistics are recorded. Lancashire cricket historian Barrie Watkins, who unearthed these figures, noted, 'He could well have been playing mainly for Gorton at this time – they were doing well in the Manchester League then, but unfortunately no individual player averages for the league were recorded in the relevant *Athletic News Cricket Annual*.'

Knocker also enjoyed running and was an accomplished billiards player. In March 1915 he was runner up in the Professional Footballers' Charity Billiards Tournament, bested only by Glossop FC's J Dearnaley.

West scored on his debut for Manchester United, on 1 September 1910, in a 2–1 win away to (Woolwich) Arsenal. He lined up – as he would all season – in the number eleven shirt, having replaced Jimmy Turnbull as United's main striking forward. United had travelled down for the match the previous day, staying overnight in a Bedford hotel and then motoring to Plumstead for the game, before returning, once again after a stop-off at Bedford.

Knocker ended the season as top scorer with nineteen goals in the League, and one in the FA Cup, missing only three of 41 League and Cup games. United had won the title for the second time. But it had been a near thing. United had started the final game of the season a point behind Aston Villa, entertaining Sunderland in front of a pessimistic crowd of 10,000. United supporters became even less optimistic when the home side went a goal down. But by half time

Turnbull, West and Harold Halse had turned the game around, putting United 3–1 up, *en route* to an eventual 5–1 triumph (a second goal for Halse, and an own goal). Meanwhile Villa had crashed to a 3–1 defeat to Liverpool.

It cost two guineas [£2.10] to buy the best Grand Stand season ticket to see Knocker in action for that campaign – although fans could purchase a Ground Only season ticket for 8s 6d [42$\frac{1}{2}$p]. The season was notable for the fact that the newly formed Players Union sought permission for their members to wear the Union's badge on their shirts, but the Football League Management Committee refused point blank. The Committee used the flimsiest of excuses to keep the players in their place – ruling that if they 'allowed the badges to be worn, unpleasantness, both among players and a section of the spectators might be caused'.

West was suspended for a month – four games – at the start of the 1911–12 season following 'an incident at Aston Villa in April 1911'. Knocker received his marching orders in front of a 55,000 crowd who witnessed 'a match that was little more than an ill-tempered battle from the first whistle to the last' and which United lost 4–2. Nevertheless West headed the club's goal-scoring list with seventeen League goals – and six more in as many FA Cup games, in a season in which United slipped to thirteenth place. West had started as centre forward in every game.

At the start of the 1912–13 season United's manager and board turned down a £1,200 offer for West from Blackburn Rovers. The second game of the season, on 7 September 1912, saw 40,000 fans swarm into Old Trafford for a United benefit (and First Division) match against neighbours City, on behalf of Billy Meredith. It earned Meredith a reported £2,000. City won 1–0. In the City side that day was Sandy Turnbull, who got involved in a fist-fight with opponent Alec Leake.

On 14 December West hammered a hat-trick as United went to Newcastle and won 3–1. He finished the 1912–13 season as the club's top scorer with twenty goals from 36 First Division outings but only found the net once in four FA Cup appearances. That season, West had appeared on the team-sheet at numbers nine and ten. His team improved to take fourth spot in the table. By 1913

West was on reported pay of £4 10s [£4.50] per week. The following year this was upped to the maximum wage of £5.

In the 1913–14 season West's goal scoring declined dramatically and his team slipped back to end in fourteenth place. He managed only half a dozen League goals from 31 appearances, while his striking colleague George Anderson grabbed fifteen goals in as many starts. West was promised a 'minimum' benefit of £500 in the 1915–16 season. That pledge would never be honoured. On 2 January 1915 United's largest crowd of the season – 31,000 spectators – was at Manchester City to see Knocker grab the goal that earned his side a 1–1 draw. The previous season United had attracted home crowds of 35,000, 36,000 and 39,000 – with up to 40,000 watching their away games.

West would end his final season with United having scored nine goals from 33 League appearances, and failing to score in their only FA Cup game that year – a 1–0 defeat away to Sheffield Wednesday. Knocker's last goal for United in a First Division game came in the penultimate game of the season, on 19 April 1915, in a 3–1 away win at Chelsea. His last outing in the competition was at home to Aston Villa on 26 April when George Anderson grabbed the only goal of the game. West's final tally with United was 72 goals from 166 League appearances, and eight goals from fifteen FA Cup starts. In the next chapter we hear how the action unfolded during the great match-rigging scandal itself.

4

Welcome to Old Trafford

'Good afternoon, and welcome to Old Trafford, for today's vital relegation showdown between traditional rivals Manchester United and Liverpool. The news from the war is mixed today, Friday – Good Friday of course – 2 April 1915. We understand that on the Western Front a German advance has been halted at Bagatelle, while French air raids have taken place on German aviation camps in Belgium. On the Eastern Front the Russian cavalry has defeated the German cavalry in northern Poland and the Russians have taken Cigielka in the Carpathians. In the North Sea, three trawlers – Jason, Gloxinia and Nellie – have been sunk by submarine U10.

The Old Trafford stadium, designed by Archibald Leitch, cost nearly £100,000 to build, and has been United's home since February 1910. Liverpool were the first visitors to play on this ground nearly five years ago when a maximum capacity crowd of 50,000 crammed in – including 5,000 or so who got in free when the turnstiles failed. Sandy Turnbull, who hasn't made the United line-up today, got the first goal of the game. The match was eventually won by the visitors. Turnbull holds the unenviable distinction of being the first Manchester United player to be sent off in a derby game, an honour he acquired back in December 1907. He was dismissed during a 3–1 home victory over Manchester City in which he had already scored twice against his old club at United's previous Hyde Road ground.

The weather has affected the turnout for today's match with only 18,000 spectators willing to brave the rain. The game gets underway at 3.30 p.m. – that's just ten minutes away now – and it doesn't look like the rain will have stopped before referee John Sharpe blows his whistle for kick off. Spectators have been sheltering from the steady downpour as they study today's match programme. No doubt they will also be discussing the news that this will be the last competitive football season until the war is over. Those players who are retained by their clubs can expect substantially reduced wages. The others will soon be out of work or facing an uncertain future, perhaps joining one of the footballers' regiments that have recruited considerable numbers of members in recent months.

In three weeks' time a capacity crowd is expected to pack into Old Trafford for the Cup Final played between Sheffield United and Chelsea. The match is already being dubbed the 'Khaki Final' as a large percentage of those in attendance are likely to be uniformed servicemen. Preparations for the final are well advanced and earlier today I spotted a couple of FA representatives – secretary Frederick Wall and up-and-coming administrator Arthur Kingscott – here to check out arrangements. I managed to get a quick word with them before they left, having clearly been deterred by the unpleasant weather from staying to watch this afternoon's game, and they assured me that everything was in hand for the big day.

There will be little love lost between these two sides today as there is a great deal at stake. United look set for the drop should they lose here but the Merseysiders themselves are not entirely free of relegation worries. United carved out a 1–1 draw at Anfield earlier in the season, on Boxing Day, just two days before their new manager, John Robson, arrived from Brighton and Hove Albion. He replaced, John J Bentley, (who went under the title of chairman and secretary) who had had to stand down owing to ill health.

There seems to be a mood of optimism among United supporters, with bookies reporting some hefty wagering in favour of the home side. There has even been a flurry of bets specifying a 2–0 victory for the home side. As a result, some 'layers' have cut their odds from 8–1 to as low as 4–1 – and I understand that one or two bookies have even declined further wagers on that particular scoreline. Although United's recent performances have been unimpressive the club have a good record against their Anfield opponents. Liverpool have failed to win at Old Trafford for the past four seasons, losing 3–0 here in the last campaign and by 3–1 in the 1912–13 season. United also won the two away fixtures against Liverpool in both of those seasons.

There is a lot of outside interest in the outcome of this match. Fred Howard and a couple of his Manchester City team-mates are here to watch the action. City, at the other end of the table, are involved in the challenge for the league title. They attracted the biggest crowd to watch United so far this year when some 30,000 spectators turned up for the local derby held at the City ground on 2 January. That match ended in a 1–1 draw, with Enoch West on target for United. I have also seen a number of other football celebrities around the ground, among them former Chester and Stockport County centre forward Lol Cook.

The teams are pretty much as predicted, although we were expecting to see Irish international Billy Lacey lining up at right half for Liverpool but I understand that former Third Lanark player Tom Fairfoul has been preferred by manager Tom Watson, who brought both of these men to Anfield. So, let's take a look at the two line-ups.

In goal for United is 31-year-old Maidstone-born Bob Beale, who was transferred from Norwich City in May 1912 for £275. He has brought to the side some much-needed reliability between the sticks, even if his defenders too often leave him exposed. Beale has also represented the Football League in a game against the Scottish League in 1913. The full backs are, on the right, John Hodge, the Stenhousemuir-born Scot, who this season has displaced his elder brother James from the position, and, on the left, Walter Spratt. Spratt, aged 22, cost United £175 when he was transferred from Brentford in February. Right half is the rugged James Montgomery, only recently joined from Second Division side Glossop, but who has already stamped his tough mark on the side. On the left is 21-year-old Joe Haywood, who cost a token fee of £50 when he moved from Hindley Central last year. Not the tallest of players at 5ft 6in, he makes up for his lack of stature with quick thinking. Centre half and captain is Dublin-born Patrick O'Connell. He cost United a substantial fee of £1,000 when he was bought from Hull City almost a year ago and has made a significant impact at the club.

Veteran player Billy Meredith, now in his forty-first year, is listed in the outside right position and the Welsh international will, no doubt, be sporting his famous trademark toothpick. He made his United debut on 1 January 1907, arriving from Manchester City where he had scored 146 goals in 339 appearances. He was no stranger to controversies of various kinds, not the least of them his notorious attempt to bribe Aston Villa skipper Alec Leake. Diminutive 26-year-old Arthur Potts, a former Willenhall Swift, will play alongside Meredith at inside right.

George Anderson, aged 22, takes the centre forward role. The locally born youngster came to United from Bury as a teenager for £50. He has been missing from the line-up since 2 January and will be keen to make an impression today having scored in four of his previous six matches before dropping out of the side. Inside left is Enoch West, better known as Knocker, who is famed for his cannonball shot. He has been a prolific scorer since transferring from Nottingham Forest for a fee rumoured to be in the region of £500. I hear West, who celebrated his twenty-ninth birthday a fortnight back, has been promised a benefit game by the club. This could prove lucrative, as Meredith made £2,000 from such a game. Completing the United line-up out is 25-year-old Joe Norton, on the left wing, who is taking over from the recently out-of-form England international George Wall. Norton signed from Nuneaton Town, having previously played for Stockport County.

Liverpool have reliable Elisha – better known as Lish – Scott in goal. Opposing forwards often make the mistake of underestimating the slim, 5ft 9in 20-year-old but he is difficult to get past. His Belfast brogue is sure to be heard this afternoon, urging on and instructing his defenders. It is a measure of boss Watson's faith in this broth of a boy that he turned down a substantial offer from Newcastle United to buy him for £1,000 two years before. His brother Billy is Everton and Ireland's goalkeeper.

At right back is the team captain, 27-year-old Bolton-born Ephraim Longworth, a versatile, frizzy haired defender, who can play on either flank. Longworth, who is tipped to receive international honours, joined the club from Southern League side Leyton in 1910. His fellow full-back is a 26-year-old Scot, Bob

Pursell (often spelled either with an 's' or a 'c'). He came to Anfield from Scottish side Queen's Park. A shade under 6ft tall, and a solid 12st in weight, Pursell has already made over one hundred appearances for the club.

In front of Pursell is 23-year-old Don McKinlay (sometimes spelled M'Kinlay). The versatile Scottish international, who joined the club from Newton Swifts in 1910, can push forward from half back to inside forward position if necessary and can pop up with the odd goal from time to time, often as a result of his awesome dead-ball strikes.

Yorkshireman, Phil Bratley, aged 24, who is enjoying his first season at Liverpool since signing from Barnsley last May, will play between the halfbacks, with Tom Fairfoul – surely one of the most comically named football players – on his right. Fairfoul, who is approaching his thirty-second birthday, joined Liverpool from Third Lanark. Seasoned campaigner Tom is a keen golfer in his spare time but will be more concerned with teeing up a winning performance this afternoon.

The diminutive John, better known as 'Jackie' (or sometimes Johnny) Sheldon – 5ft 6½in tall – lines up on the right wing against his former side. Born in 1888 in Clay Cross, near Chesterfield, he joined Liverpool from United eighteen months before. He may have been tired of acting as understudy to Billy Meredith, who he confronts this afternoon. Sheldon has replaced Arthur Goddard in the Liverpool side. Another relatively short player, Northumbrian Willie Banks, 22, who is a shade under 5ft 7in, will assume the inside forward role alongside Sheldon, with the two-inch taller Fred Pagnam spearheading the forward line. Poulton-Le-Fylde born Fred, 22, is a much-travelled player, having performed for Sheffield Wednesday, Huddersfield, Southport Central and Blackpool. Son of a bank manager, Fred will be hoping to create interest in his performance today. The pacey 24-year-old Tom Miller will play on Pagnam's left. The 5ft 9in tall Miller has been with Liverpool just over two years. He joined the club for a fee of £400 from Hamilton. He clearly wasn't signed to appeal to lady spectators – I have to say that from a particular angle Miller could be mistaken for that poor unfortunate of recent public renown, who was known by the sobriquet 'Elephant Man'. Miller's brother John has also played for Liverpool.

Completing the line-up is Jimmy Nicholl at left wing. Defenders have learned to fear the strength of Nicholl's left foot – so powerful that Burnley's Taylor was knocked out when he headed a goal-bound effort from Nicholl off the line in last season's FA Cup Final. Nicholl is one of several members of that Cup Final side (which Liverpool lost 1–0 to Burnley) who is turning out today – the others being Miller, Sheldon, McKinlay, Fairfoul, Pursell and Longworth.

The referee, John Sharpe, of Lichfield, is not the most experienced of match officials. Sharpe is in his first full season at the first class level and is on the supplementary – rather than the main – list. He was involved in a controversial incident last December when he was fined half a guinea for failing to turn up for a match at Aston Villa. The teams have now taken the field. The home side has won the toss and now both sides are positioning themselves ready for kick off. It is now time to hand you over to my colleague for the full match commentary...

Red-shirted United are playing with the breeze behind them, which is gusting the heavy rain into the faces of the visitors. Liverpool are playing in their change strip colours of white shirts and black shorts... United, on the attack from the very start, have just won a corner, which the moustachioed Meredith is shaping up to take. Over it comes, swinging in towards the goal where Scott, with his always slicked-back hair plastered to his head by the driving rain, is beaten as the ball bounces off the bar and falls behind the goal – that was close. Lish is already struggling to maintain his usual immaculate appearance...

Scott takes the goal kick but United quickly win the ball back and attack again. Now Montgomery has collected the ball, displaying delightful footwork to clear space for himself before hitting a tremendous effort into the well-positioned Scott's hands. The ball is cleared away from the Liverpool goal – but not for long. Here's left winger Norton on the run, hitting a shot that has beaten Scott – only to rebound back from the post. Liverpool are living dangerously here and the home side is keen to establish early superiority. Now it is United pushing forward again and the ball is played through to Anderson whose shot is beaten out by Scott, who reacts quickly to save the follow-up effort from the same forward ... West has worked his way into a shooting position – only to find Scott equal to his effort...

With almost half an hour played, Scott has been the busiest man on the park so far. At the other end, Beale, who has been present in all of his side's 32 matches – except for the visit of Burnley in mid November – is having the quietest afternoon of his season, quiet enough for him to light up a cigarette and take it up to his chain-smoking counterpart at the other end of the pitch. The weather, though, has improved somewhat with the heavy rain easing off and a little sunshine putting in a welcome appearance...

Liverpool's midfield players have been battling hard to contain the United forwards but have been unable to create any aggressive moves of their own, and we have seen little sign of McKinlay's trademark overlapping runs on the flanks. Now here's a chance for Pagnam to break through – oh! good tackle from O'Connell, which stops the Liverpool man in his tracks...

Anderson is dribbling his way into a promising situation and he whacks a shot at point-blank range straight at the alert Scott. The Liverpool keeper can only parry the ball to the feet of the onrushing West, who must surely convert the chance – but, my word, he has hit the ball wide. Scott is called into the action yet again, as Potts shoots goalwards. Scott is down to make a save, but Anderson seems to be claiming the ball has crossed the goal-line. The referee, Sharpe, disagrees and rules against him. (The official is certainly having to work hard to earn his £1 11/6d [£1.57p] fee – not to mention the third-class railway fare to which he is entitled-for officiating at this game.)

Liverpool's Nicholl and Sheldon are now winning the ball in midfield and have each put in a couple of good centres, but neither of them has yet found the head or feet of Pagnam, the long-faced Miller, or Banks in a position that will enable them to put Beale under pressure...

Liverpool have just repelled a series of four consecutive corners into their goal area, but despite all the Manchester United huffing and puffing, it looks as though the visitors will hold out until half time – just five minutes away. But wait – Montgomery has won the ball and played it through from his position on the right to find George Anderson who doesn't hesitate but drives a firm volley into the far corner of the net, well out of reach of Scott's despairing dive, to give United a dramatic lead. The goal delights the home supporters who applaud enthusiastically and wave their caps in the air. This could be just the tonic United need to push forward and register the emphatic victory that their domination has deserved...

Liverpool have finally roused themselves and are enjoying a brief period of aggressive play just before the interval. But although they are managing to gain possession in the middle of the pitch they are unable to create any genuine alarm among the home rearguard. Referee Sharpe blows his whistle and the sides head back to their dressing rooms. The Manchester United players are probably regretting that they have but one goal to show for their unusually dominant display and the Liverpool squad will be anxious to regroup, change tactics and begin to have an influence on a match that seems to be slipping away from their grasp...

You rejoin us for the second half of this intriguing clash between Manchester United and Liverpool in which so much is at stake. We understand that there has been something of an altercation within the visitors' dressing room en route to which, a number of the Liverpool players were actually heard threatening not to reappear for the second half. They must be seriously disgruntled with their performance. This does not augur well for an improved level of teamwork among the Mersey men in the second period of play.

I can now see the two sides returning to the pitch – and both have their full complement of players, so presumably manager Tom Watson has managed to placate his men...

As the second half kicks off, Manchester United are again making all the running... Anderson hits a goal-bound shot from close range and Scott leaps to push it over the crossbar... Once more the ball finds its way into the Liverpool penalty area where, if I am not much mistaken, Bob Pursell, easily recognisable by that thick dark hair with its distinctive centre parting, has just handled the ball deliberately – what will the referee decide? He seems to be in no doubt. Just under five minutes into the second half, Mr Sharpe points towards the spot, awarding a penalty kick to the home side. Anderson is usually charged with responsibility for such situations, but is making no effort to come forward. Anderson is clearly in form, having already scored and this could be a vital chance for United to put the game out of Liverpool's reach. If the ball does not go in, it could ignite Liverpool's belief that they can still save the game. This is strange. It appears as though Patrick O'Connell has picked up the pigskin and is intending to take the shot. He runs up to take the kick – oh no! I can barely believe my eyes – he has completely missed his shot, putting the ball yards wide of the post. Even Beale in the United goal looks as though he cannot believe what he has just seen. O'Connell himself seems completely unfazed – you'd almost think he was smiling from the look on his face which is, admittedly, some considerable distance away from me... If I didn't know better, I'd be thinking that he'd done that on purpose.

Referee Sharpe is consulting with his linesman, Hargreaves – I've no idea what they can be discussing. There seemed to have been no infringement from the other players. Scott did not move or distract O'Connell as he ran in to kick the ball. The officials now finish their discussions and the game resumes with a goal kick.

The ground is still buzzing as spectators endeavour to make sense of what they have just seen... The crowd seems somewhat baffled by this turn of events and there is a certain amount of consternation and apparent discontent...

At last Liverpool are showing a flash of defiance. Pagnam, who has been ineffective for most of the game, heads dangerously just over the United bar – the ball may even have just made glancing contact with the woodwork – an excellent effort that, strangely, seems to attract little approval from his colleagues. One or two of them seem to look positively annoyed with their colleague – yet he was in a better position to head for goal than towards one of his team-mates so I cannot understand their irritation...

For the past quarter of an hour play has really gone flat with very little in the way of incident or action. Oddly enough, Liverpool do not seem to have galvanised themselves significantly since the missed penalty, and the United defence is comfortably dealing with the best the visitors can offer. The best efforts on the Liverpool side are coming from Sheldon, who is showing good footwork and crossing ability but without giving Beale much cause for concern...

Now Spratt demonstrates United's totally comfortable attitude at the back by neatly flicking the ball over Sheldon's head before clearing it away. West seems to have dropped back into a deeper role this half. His ankles are strapped, perhaps he is carrying an injury.

We are now moving into the final quarter of the game and Manchester United are mounting an attack led by O'Connell. The ball is being played by Norton into a dangerous position in front of Scott – a mêlée of players is tussling for the ball, with the keeper desperate to get hold of it. Scott gets a hand to the ball, only to divert it into the path of Anderson. The centre forward lashes out to hit the ball goalwards through the ruck of bodies and – yes! – the ball is in the back of the net. This is Anderson's second goal of the game and it gives United a 2–0 lead. United are delighted, but Liverpool are less than pleased – as are, I should imagine, those bookmakers who have apparently accepted a substantial number of bets on a 2–0 victory for the home side. With around fifteen minutes of the match remaining, there is still time for the score to change. Perhaps Anderson will complete his hat-trick...

United seem to have settled for the win now and are keen not to allow Liverpool any opportunity to sneak back into the game by attacking too recklessly thus allowing the visitors to hit back on the break – the deep lying West is now proving most effective in lustily clearing the ball into touch whenever it comes near him – a ploy suggested, or instructed, by his skipper, I should think.

Now I can bring you some sensational news – I am being told that the United manager, John Robson, has been seen departing the ground – what can this mean? Does he have an appointment that is so important that he cannot remain to congratulate his victorious men? Is he dissatisfied with his team's performance this afternoon? I imagine the indifferent display of the Liverpool side will do little to improve the disposition of their manager Tom Watson who reportedly has not been a well man of late...

Mr Sharpe consults his time-piece and decides that ninety minutes has elapsed, so Manchester United can start to celebrate the two points that may yet keep them in the First Division. One might have expected unalloyed delight from the home supporters for such a great result but I have heard one or two rumbles of discontent and there have even been shouts from the crowd to the effect that the result was rigged – I heard one or two people calling 'play the game, United' earlier on – and it has to be said that a neutral observer might be forgiven for concluding that only one of the sides cared about the outcome of this afternoon's game. A man on his way out of the ground has just said to me: 'You don't need the war to stop the game – football of this sort will do it soon enough.' Far be it from me to suggest that anything untoward has occurred this afternoon, but the authorities may reflect that Liverpool were involved in two previous inquiries into games suspected of being conducted in – shall we say – an unsatisfactory manner, although they were subsequently absolved of any wrongdoing. On that grave note I hand you back to my colleagues in the studio . . . '

5

Players in the Drama

Several key figures had a part to play in the infamous events that
unfolded at Old Trafford on that fateful day. Not all of them had
been on the pitch – and not all of them were suspended. Some
players, such as George Anderson, Billy Meredith and Patrick
O'Connell, were never directly implicated in the plot. Yet it is
difficult to believe they were not aware of events that day and did
not play some part in the proceedings. The players who would
receive bans – in addition to Enoch West – were Sandy Turnbull and
Arthur Whalley, of Manchester United, neither of whom played in
the game; Tom Fairfoul, Tom Miller, Bob Purcell and Jackie
Sheldon of Liverpool; Fred Howard of Manchester City and –
perhaps most mysteriously of all – Lol Cook of Chester.

Lawrence ('Lol') Whalley Cook is believed to have been born in
Preston on 28 March 1885 (surely, entirely coincidental that he
shared a name with another of the players suspended for life –
Arthur Whalley?). Lol's first significant sporting achievement was
to make his First Class debut for Lancashire County Cricket Club in
the 'War of the Roses' showdown against Yorkshire at Old Trafford
in 1907. Cook made an immediate impact, dismissing Yorkshire
batsman Wilfred Rhodes with his first ball.

An accomplished all-rounder, Cook joined Chester FC from
Bacup at the start of the 1911–12 season, and scored 36 league goals
in 32 Lancashire Combination Division One games, playing in
every game of the season. In the programme for the Chester versus
St Helens Town game of 9 September 1911, Cook received a

glowing description – despite his chronic bashfulness. The programme writer stated:

> This player is so shy that I have not been able to persuade him to give me short particulars of his football career. All the same, he will have to run the gauntlet, for when the Editor makes up his mind to fix [*ironic choice of word?* – GS] a player in the Photo Gallery his wish must be obeyed. Mr Cook, I humbly apologise for this publicity, but it is not my fault. To those who follow cricket, Cook needs little introduction, for his deeds in the cricketing world are well known. Lancashire possess few better bowlers, and Captain Hornby might do worse than give him a more extended trial. On the football field Cook is equally well known, and his display on our ground when playing for Bacup is not forgotten. That day he and 'A J' had a duel royal, and methinks friend Cook had just a wee bit better of the deal. We sadly needed a clever, bustling centre forward and in Cook we have the genuine article. Dashing, daring, and a deadly shot, it behoves defenders to look out for trouble when he is on the war path. His turn of speed for one so bulky (pardon the phrase) is surprising and he possesses the happy knack of distributing the ball impartially, thus opening out the game to the enjoyment of spectators and the consternation of opponents. The Chester crowd love an all-round sport and Cook will soon find himself a popular idol. May his connection with the Club be a long and happy one.

But it was not to be – at the end of the season Cook joined Stockport County, then in Division Two, and scored four goals in ten League games, including a hat-trick on his debut. He also scored twice in two FA Cup matches. Cook re-joined Chester (they did not append the 'City' until 1983) for the 1913–14 season and added another ten goals in fifteen games. But he was no longer the same player, the reason, perhaps, being revealed in the Chester programme for another match against St Helens Town. Almost two years to the day since his first appearance for the club had been recorded, this programme stated that Cook had been 'struck down with a severe illness from which he did not altogether recover until the spring'.

Chester archivist Chas Sumner told me, 'Glancing through programmes for the 1913–14 season I get the impression that he was not playing that well, and Chester finished the season in twelfth place out of eighteen. It also seems that at the end of the season only two players were retained – and Cook was not one of them. Certainly Cook made no appearances in the 1914–15 season, and Chester withdrew their membership from the Lancashire Combination in March, before the infamous Manchester United–Liverpool game. I suspect that by 1915 Cook had probably finished playing, but Chester were registered as his last club.'

I have been unable to trace any record of Lol Cook making further appearances for any senior sides. However, details discovered by Michael Joyce, who has been researching pre-war players, suggest that Cook may also have played for Nelson, Blackpool, Preston (1905–6) and possibly Gainsborough Trinity (1908).

Lol's brother William also played for Preston and Oldham, and appeared for the Football League in 1919. William was involved in one of the most bizarre of all football incidents just three days after the Manchester United–Liverpool game. Playing for Oldham at Middlesbrough on Easter Monday, Cook was sent off by referee H Smith of Nottingham in the second half when his team was 4–1 down. William Cook refused point-blank to go, whereupon the referee walked off and abandoned the game. Cook was subsequently banned for a year. This could not have been an attempt to distract attention from another, more sinister, controversy involving his brother... could it? Maybe not, but Lancashire County Cricket Club Librarian Barrie Watkins says that, like his brother, William was a cricketer, making eleven appearances for Lancashire between 1905–7. According to Barrie, William's overall sporting conduct made 'Roy Keane look like Mother Theresa!'

Lol Cook's cricketing career comfortably outclassed his footballing achievements, but few chroniclers of his role in the Manchester United–Liverpool affair have paid him much attention, probably because there seemed to be nothing to link him directly with the other accused players.

Cook played 203 times for the County, between 1907 and 1923. As a star Lancashire CCC player, Cook may well have offered the plotters a way of diverting attention away from the source of the bets going on the 2–0 scoreline. Perhaps he become pally with Enoch West when the United man was briefly on the cricket club's books. Cricketers have traditionally enjoyed a gamble and would probably have attracted little initial attention or comment when placing a bet. Lol could well have been a very useful third party, capable of staking the money for the schemers, with Enoch acting as the go-between even if he had declined to become directly involved himself. Alternatively, perhaps Enoch arranged for Cook to put on the bets, in return for a cut of the profits.

Lol's association with the scandal seems not to have had an adverse effect on his standing in the cricket world. Barrie Watkins told me, 'I have checked every history of Lancashire CCC from the nineteen-twenties until today and his football is not mentioned, unlike his brother's. Strange.'

To this day, Lancashire remains proud of its black sheep – the club's web-site records that in 1920 Lancashire finished runners-up to Middlesex in the Championship. 'Attendances were good during the year with Harry Dean and Lol Cook getting 274 wickets between them.' Seven of those wickets were taken by the latter in a game at Chesterfield against Derbyshire when Lol conceded just eight runs in a brilliant fourteen-over spell.

Nor was Lol a flash in the pan. The *Wisden Book of Obituaries* said he 'did his best work after the War, his last four seasons being his most successful'. In 1920 Lol took 156 wickets at an outstanding average of 14.88. In 1921 he chalked up his best batting performance, hitting 54 not out against Middlesex at Old Trafford. During the same season he stunned Northants by taking eight for 39 on their ground. He was, during this campaign, selected for the Players at Lord's and ended the season with 151 wickets at an average of 22.99 runs per wicket.

The Lancashire website also records that, in 1922, as Lancashire finished fifth, 'Cec Parkin took 172 wickets, splendidly supported by Lol Cook with 136' (although Wisden credits him with 142 at an average of 22). In 1923 Cook took 98 wickets, and made a reported

£1,650 from his benefit, and then became a professional with Rawtenstall Cricket Club.

Lol Cook died at Mesnes, Wigan, on 2 December 1933 at the relatively young age (particularly for a former sportsman) of 48.

Alexander ('Sandy') Turnbull was born in Hurlford, near Kilmarnock, in 1884, the second of seven children, for Jessie and, yes, James! An inside forward, his fierce playing style earned him the nickname 'Turnbull the Terrible'. Abandoning his working life as a coal miner, he joined Manchester City in 1902 from Hurlford Thistle (despite having earlier given his word to join Bolton Wanderers) where he scored sixty goals in 119 games. Turnbull moved to Manchester United in 1906 following a scandal for which seventeen City players – of whom he was one and Billy Meredith another – were suspended for accepting illegal payments.

At 5ft 7in tall and weighing around 12st, Turnbull was a very solid-looking figure. A terrific header of the ball, Turnbull scored the only goal on his 1 January 1907 debut against Aston Villa at Old Trafford. He became top scorer in United's 1907–8 first League title winning side with 25 goals. His place in Manchester United folklore was assured when he scored the first ever competitive goal at Old Trafford, on 19 February 1910, against Liverpool. However, the Merseysiders went on to win the match 4–3, in front of a crowd estimated at 50,000 although 'a few thousand' more were reckoned to have sneaked in illicitly.

Turnbull is Manchester United's twelfth most prolific all-time scorer with a total of one hundred goals for the club. These came in 245 League games (scoring ninety goals) and 25 Cup matches (scoring ten goals) and included the winning goal in the 1909 FA Cup Final against Bristol City. To celebrate that victory, Turnbull and team-mates went to the Alhambra Theatre to see renowned comedian George Robey. Spirits were high and the FA Cup was passed around from player to player, only for its lid to go missing – turning up the next morning in Turnbull's jacket pocket where a team joker had secreted it. During the First World War Turnbull played for both Rochdale and Clapton Orient.

One incident in particular, in a match against Oldham on 19 November 1910, in which he scored two of the three goals in the 3–1 win, really captured Turnbull's rebellious spirit. Turnbull was cautioned for making remarks to the referee who warned him that he would be sent off if he repeated the offending phrase. At the end of the match, Turnbull approached the referee, who had been expecting an apology, and told him, 'I only wanted to tell you that I have said it again, but you didn't hear me.'

Turnbull boasts a bizarre claim to soccer immortality as perhaps the first footballer ever eulogised in verse or song. It came about as a result of the 1909 FA Cup Final between Manchester United and Bristol City when Turnbull was a doubtful starter following an injury scare. United skipper Charlie Roberts reportedly said, 'Let him play. He might get a goal and if he does we can afford to carry a passenger.' [No subs in those days – GS] After the match *Athletic News* carried a specially composed poem or song called 'Sandy' in tribute to him:

> Why, we thought that you were crocked, Dashing Sandy
> That to fame your road was blocked, Hard lines Sandy
> But you came up to the scratch
> Made an effort for THE match
> A great victory to snatch – Bravo Sandy
> When you beat the Stalwart City, Shooting Sandy
> Topping off a glorious day, Blithesome Sandy
> We could scarce believe our eyes
> It was such a glad surprise
> But of course you ne'er loved ties, Did you Sandy?
> When Fales hit the shiv-ring bar, Lucky Sandy
> There were groans heard near and far, Deep ones Sandy
> But the ball was on the bound
> And your boot was safe and sound
> When the net your great shot found, Champion Sandy
> Well United owe the Cup, To you Sandy
> For the score was but one up – not much Sandy?
> But the Bristol boys worked hard
> Though their efforts were ill-starred
> Give a cheer then with the bard, For them Sandy

In April 1914 Turnbull and George Stacey were granted a benefit match – a derby against Manchester City which raised the pair receipts of £1,216. This was to be shared between them – assuming they received the cash. In December 1916 the *Manchester Football Chronicle* reported, 'There is still benefit money owing to Meredith and other players who have not had the whole of the money due to them.'

In October 1915 (by which time the First World War had finally led to the closure of League football) Turnbull was working for the Ship Canal Company, putting in 'some long hours and good work' according to local reports, which added, 'He was working on one of the sugar boats last week.' Sandy decided to join the Footballers Battalion in November 1915. A *Manchester Football News* columnist declared, 'He has more to sacrifice than many men I know.' Before meeting a tragic end himself, Turnbull experienced an horrific incident which must have been all too common for soldiers fighting in the war. In a letter back to his one time United skipper, Charlie Roberts, Turnbull wrote:

Did you receive a letter with some things which a pal and I took from a lad who was lying in front of our trench? I have been wondering if you knew him and if his relations are about Clayton. It was a start to me when I turned the poor lad over and saw he belonged to the district of Manchester. It brought back memories of many a happy day. We buried him as decently as we could. I stuck a bit of wood with his name and number at the top of the grave.

In September 1916 Sandy was keeping his spirits up according to the *Manchester Football Chronicle*, which reported, 'Sandy Turnbull is evidently the same quiet humorist as a soldier as he was when the life and soul of the Manchester United party on their travels. I hear he has written home, saying that he has had a game of football and has not slept since because he 'forgot to ask the permission of the FA'.

Would Chronicle writer, 'Wanderer', really have been this affectionate towards Turnbull had he genuinely believed him to be a prime mover in a dastardly plot to undermine the sport of football? Six weeks later the *Chronicle* again mentioned Sandy, who had sent 'a letter home, full of humour and very cheery.'

He met a sad end on 3 May 1917, killed in action at Arras, France. The story of Turnbull's death is typical of many such tragic tales from the 'Great War'. Although he had been reported missing and wounded it wasn't known for sure what had happened to him until his commanding officer, Captain C J Lonergan of the 8th East Battalion Surrey Regiment returned to England having been held prisoner in Germany. He wrote to Lance Sergeant Turnbull's wife in August 1918:

It was a great shock to me to hear that my best NCO, i.e. Sergeant Turnbull, was still missing. Of course, I knew there was no hope of him turning up after such a long period. He was one of the finest fellows I have ever met. A great sportsman and as keen a soldier as he was a footballer. He had been hit through the leg early on in the fight. When I saw him his leg was very much swollen, so I ordered him back to the dressing station. He pleaded so hard, however, to be allowed to stay on until we had gained our objective that I gave way. Sandy was in command of a platoon. The men would simply go anywhere with him. Well, the end of it all was that, although we gained all our objectives, the division on our left did not. Consequently, the enemy got round on our flanks and we had to get back as best we could. We came under very heavy machine-gun fire during the withdrawal. This was when I was hit. As I fell I saw your husband pass me a few yards away. I saw him get to the village which we had taken that morning. There was some shelter here from the bullets so I heaved a sigh of relief when I saw him disappear among the houses. I knew he could get back to our lines with comparative safety from there. I never heard anything more of him. Those who were wounded all thought that Sandy had got back. It was a bitter disappointment to me to hear that he had not been heard of. The only explanation I can give is that he must have been 'sniped' by a German who was lying low in one of the houses. It was a rotten bit of luck. I would have recommended him from

Germany, but I had my doubts whether the German Censor would allow it to come through. However, I put his case strongly when I wrote from Holland and I do hope that he will get the highest distinction possible. He certainly deserves it.

With a touch of hypocrisy, *Athletic News*, which had previously pilloried Turnbull and his fellow suspended professionals, declared, 'The football world will read this tribute from Captain Cecil J Lonergan with intense interest and hope that his gallant bearing in the face of death will be recognised. All those who ever played with Sandy Turnbull will not be in the least surprised at the admiration of his company commander.'

Billy Meredith's biographer John Harding called Turnbull, a father of four, 'A colourful, if at times rather dubious character', and 'one of the best Scottish inside forwards never to have played for his country'. In August 1932 two of Sandy's sons, Alexander and Ronald, signed as amateurs for Manchester United, though neither made a first-team appearance. Turnbull's name is commemorated on a huge war memorial located on the outskirts of Arras in northern France.

Arthur Whalley was born in Rainford, Lancashire on 17 February 1886. He was bought by Manchester United for £50 in 1909, arriving from Blackpool where he had played just five games (scoring twice). Whalley broke through into Manchester United's first team on the departure of Charlie Roberts to Oldham, making his debut at Sheffield Wednesday on 27 December 1909. A 5ft 8in, 11st 10lb centre half, he won a League Championship medal in 1910–11, having made 15 appearances. During the 1912–13 season he represented the Football League against the Irish League, but suffered a serious knee injury, after taking part in a North versus South international trial, and played just once during the 1914–15 season.

During the early part of the First World War, Whalley was reported by the *Manchester Football Chronicle* of 27 November 1915 to be, 'playing splendidly in the south. He has astonished a good many people by the class of his work at Clapton Orient recently'. Whalley joined the Middlesex Regiment, where he reached the rank of sergeant, before being seriously wounded at the Battle of Passchendaele. He resumed his career at Manchester after his suspension was lifted and in total played one hundred games for the club, netting half a dozen times. He departed for Southend United in 1920 for a fee of £1,000 when Manchester United would not offer him a benefit game. He played thirty games for Southend (scoring five goals) before moving to Charlton (88 games and eight goals) and Millwall (eight games). He finished his footballing career as trainer/coach at Barrow – even playing once – in 1926. Intriguingly, Whalley went on to become a bookmaker in Manchester. He died in that city on 23 November 1952 aged 66.

Fred Howard was born in Walkden, Greater Manchester in 1893. He began his football career with Walkden Wednesday in 1912, moving to Manchester City as an amateur on 18 September 1912 and signing as a professional on 10 October of that year. In his prime he stood just over 5ft 10in tall and weighed 12st 6lb. He played for Manchester City in two spells between 1912 and 1920, making 79 League appearances (and scoring forty goals), playing ten FA Cup games (where he notched up three goals), plus making seven other appearances (which produced four goals). In total he made 96 appearances and scored 47 goals. He also played 27 games for the Reserves, scoring thirteen goals.

Howard was one of very few players to score four goals on his League debut, doing so in City's 4–0 victory over Liverpool on 18 January 1913 – having grabbed a hat-trick within thirteen minutes. He then scored in each of his next two games against Bolton and Sheffield United. Howard was suspended for 'insubordination' during City's 4–1 League defeat away to Aston Villa on 21 April 1915. On 16 October 1915, the *Manchester Football Chronicle* reported that Howard 'appeared before the FA Commission in Manchester [presumably to answer questions about the infamous Good Friday United–Liverpool game – GS] and succeeded in his application to take part in certain matches'. During the First World War, the *Chronicle* added that 'Howard is working on munitions'. Later Howard joined Mid Rhondda, Pontypridd, Gillingham, Dundee, Hibernian, Ayr, Clyde, Port Vale, New Brighton, Wrexham and Welshpool, finally finishing his lengthy career at Holyhead Town in January 1926. Gary James, the Manchester City archivist helpfully 'managed to dig out' some of these details for me, including the information that Howard was known as 'Pant' – 'for some obscure reason'.

Jackie Sheldon was born in Clay Cross, near Chesterfield, in 1887 or 1888. He started out with Nuneaton Town and then moved to Manchester United, where he made 26 League appearances and scored once, in November 1913. He was unable, though, to oust Billy Meredith from the side. A right winger, he later joined Liverpool, where he played a total of 129 games and netted seventeen or twenty goals (depending on which records you believe). He finally retired through injury in 1922. He was probably the ring-leader for the betting scam. The *Anfield Encyclopaedia* said, 'Sheldon was rumoured to have acted as go-between when Liverpool and Manchester United players fixed the result'. He died on 19 March 1941 aged 53.

Patrick O'Connell was born in Dublin on 8 March 1887. He played for Strandville Junior Team before joining Belfast Celtic in 1908, and then going on to Sheffield Wednesday in 1909. He remained there until 1912, when he joined Hull City, arriving at Old Trafford in June 1913 and becoming the skipper. After the War, during which he made guest appearances for Rochdale and Clapton Orient, he played in a Victory International against Scotland and then joined Dumbarton.

O'Connell later became player-manager at Ashington, and when the money ran out there he went off to Spain, playing for sides as diverse as Santander and Real Madrid, before coaching 1934–5 League champions Betis Balonpie. He then joined Barcelona, returning to Ireland in 1938 as Catalunia broke down in the chaos of the Spanish Civil War, only to head back to Spain from 1940–45, during the Second World War, where he was with FC Sevilla. O'Connell died on February 27, 1959, aged 71.

Billy 'Prince of Dribblers' Meredith was born in Chirk, near Wrexham, on 28 July 1874. In 1905, as skipper of Manchester City, Meredith was banned for twelve months after trying to bribe Aston

Villa captain Alec Leake £10 to throw a game, which City lost 3–2. Meredith initially claimed he was completely innocent, but later confessed his guilt. City manager Tony Maley was banned for life and other players were fined. Meredith later joined Manchester United where he made 303 League starts and scored 35 goals. Apart from a brief return to Manchester City during the First World War (and despite a dispute over benefit money), Meredith stayed with Manchester United until 1921, when – at the age of 46 – he was given a free transfer. He then became player-coach at Manchester City, where he would eventually total 366 League matches and score 145 goals. In 1924, in his fiftieth year, Meredith played in the FA Cup semifinal when City lost 2–0 to Newcastle. Meredith also earned 48 caps for Wales during his long career. He returned to United as coach before retiring from football in 1931 to run a pub (the Stretford Road Hotel, in Manchester), a cinema and a sports outfitter's shop. He also worked as a radio broadcaster for many years. Meredith died on 19 April 1958 in Withington, Manchester, aged 83.

George Anderson was born in Cheetham (appropriately enough?) in 1893. He played three games for Bury in the 1909–10 season before leaving for Manchester United, where he scored 37 goals in eighty games. In February 1916 he moved to Ireland to play for Belfast United, without mentioning the fact to his employers, Manchester United, who were not best pleased. United notified the Football League, who blocked the move. Two years later Anderson was jailed for eight months following serious accusations of fraud in connection with betting on matches.

Tom Fairfoul was born in West Calder, Midlothian on 16 January 1881. He joined Third Lanark in 1906, at right half, having earlier played for Kilmarnock. Fairfoul transferred to Liverpool in 1913, playing for them in the 1914 Cup Final – one of a total of 62 appearances for the club. In his prime Fairfoul was 5ft 9¹/₂in tall and weighed 11st 10lb. His suspension following the inquiry into the Good Friday game effectively killed off his career, as he was already 34 years old when it was imposed. He later became a 'taxi proprietor' in Liverpool. He died in 1952.

Tom Miller was born in Motherwell on 29 June 1890. In eight years Miller played 146 times for Liverpool, netting 58 goals – sixteen of them in 1913-14, his best season. He also played for Liverpool in the 1914 FA Cup Final. In 1920 he signed for Manchester United, staying for just one season and playing 27 games and scoring eight goals. He was a Scottish international centre forward who was capped once for his country while at Liverpool and twice more with Manchester United. He was 5ft 9in and weighed 11st 4lb in his prime. Miller transferred to Hearts in 1921, for £550, and then moved on to Torquay for the 1922–3 season, before joining Hamilton Academicals for £100 in 1923 and ending up at Raith Rovers for the 1926–7 season. Miller was a member of a footballing family. His brother John was also a Liverpool player, and John and four cousins played for Hamilton Academicals. He was uncle of Scotland cap, John Govan, a right back who played for Hibernian and Ayr. Tom died on 3 September 1958.

Robert ('Bob') Russell Pursell was born on 18 March 1889 in Campbeltown, Argyll. He played first for Aberdeen University, and later moved to Liverpool from Scottish side Queens Park in September 1911. The transfer was somewhat controversial because, although Liverpool approached the player, they neglected to mention their interest in him to his club, an oversight that earned them a fine of £250. Full back Pursell played 112 times for Liverpool, and after the First World War, moved to Port Vale, where he partnered his elder brother Peter, a Scottish international. The pair, who wed sisters, also teamed up to run a Hanley tobacconist's business for 43 years until they both retired in 1965. Bob died on 24 May 1974, aged 85.

6

Suspicion Grows

The reports of the match published in the following day's newspapers gave generally unflattering pictures of the displays by both teams, but there were few indications that the sports writers had noticed anything blatantly untoward on the field of play. On Saturday 3 April 1915 the *Sporting Chronicle* carried its report of the match (along with advertisements for some twenty bookmakers, whose addresses were as far apart as Southport and Basle). First, the *Chronicle* listed the players. The Manchester United line up was: Robert 'Bob' Beale (goalkeeper); James Hodge (right back); Walter Spratt (left back); James Montgomery (right half); Patrick O'Connell (centre half); Joe Haywood (left half); Billy Meredith (outside right); Arthur Potts (inside right); George Anderson (centre forward); Enoch 'Knocker' West (inside left); Joe Norton (outside left).

The Liverpool players were listed as: Elisha Scott (goalkeeper); Ephraim Longworth (right back); Robert Pursell (left back); Thomas Fairfoul (right half); Phil Bratley (centre half); Donald McKinlay (or M'Kinlay, left half); Jackie Sheldon (outside right); Willie Banks (inside right); Frederick Pagnam (centre forward); Thomas Miller (inside left); James Nicholl (outside left). Interestingly, Fairfoul had kept his place, despite the *Sporting Chronicle* forecasting that he would lose out to Billy Lacey.

The referee was given as I G A Sharpe of Lichfield. The initial 'I' was a mistake as his Christian name was John. The linesmen's names were not given. The *Sporting Chronicle*'s match report

appeared under the scintillating heading 'A Moderate Game –
Manchester United Get Two Points From Liverpool':

Heavy rain at noon spoiled the 'gate' at Old Trafford. Rain also
fell heavily in the first few minutes of the game, but later the
afternoon turned out beautifully fine. Under the circumstances
an attendance of 15,000 was all that could be expected. The
home side had a breeze behind them in the opening half and had
much the best of the play, Meredith hitting the bar from a corner
kick and a hot shot by Norton rebounding from the far post.
Nicholl and Sheldon at times broke away and invariably centred
well, but Beale was not troubled, O'Connell simply smothering
Pagnam five minutes before the interval. Montgomery, who
played finely all through the half, passed to Anderson, and the
United centre forward volleyed the ball clean into the net. This
was a beautiful shot, and prior to it, as showing the superiority
of the home side, they had taken four corner kicks in succession.
In the second half the play fell off greatly, the forwards on both
sides being slow and unenthusiastic. The game for a long time
was decidedly dull and the crowd were very silent until
Anderson rushed a second goal for the home side. The Liverpool
forwards gave the weakest exhibition in this half seen on the
ground during the season.

    Prior to the second goal, by the way, O'Connell had shot
yards wide from a penalty kick to the home side for hands
against Pursell. The play in the concluding stages was too
poor to describe. Beale in the home goal had not a good shot
to parry in all the match. Hodge played sturdily but Spratt
was the best back on the field, tackling and kicking with
finish and strength.

    Montgomery in the first half was the best man on the field
and generally the United were the superior set, Anderson being
a decided success as the leader of the forward line. The
Liverpool backs, M'Kinlay [sic] at left half back and Sheldon
and Nicholl were the most prominent on the visiting side. As
has already been indicated the proceedings in the second half
reflected no credit to either side.

The reported crowd of 15,000 (different sources would vary between 10,000–18,000) compared well with an average attendance for the season of 11,950, which ranked them only fifteenth. This was a huge drop from the previous season's 25,515, when United had been the fourth-best-supported side in the division.

Other reports of the match suggested that elements in the crowd voiced their opinion that the game was rigged, and Liverpool's Fred Pagnam was said to have been chastised by a colleague after hitting the bar. Fate was certainly unkind to all the players on the pitch at that moment. Had Pagnam's effort found its way into the United net the bookmakers would not have had to pay out on a 2–0 scoreline and the match would have been quickly forgotten. Although a few rumours might still have circulated suggesting that Liverpool had not played to their usual standard, it is unlikely the match would have stayed in the public's consciousness for long as it did. Perhaps, too, with a Liverpool goal in the scoreline, Sandy Turnbull's life would have taken a different turn and his end might have been delayed by many years. Enoch West would almost certainly have continued playing for seasons to come. But it was not to be. Pagnam's shot on goal, without the advantage of the light, easily curved footballs of today, was a matter of inches from changing history.

The referee was quoted as calling the game 'the most extraordinary match I have ever officiated in'. It later emerged that he and linesman Fred Hargreaves had discussed their suspicions about the conduct of the game on the pitch after Patrick O'Connell, United's Irish international skipper, had put his penalty unfeasibly wide of the post. Some reports later claimed that Anderson was the regular penalty taker, just to add one more suspicious aspect to that afternoon's events. United expert Iain McCartney wrote in 1996, 'To the crowd's amazement, centre half O'Connell stepped up to take the kick instead of the regular penalty taker Anderson.'

The linesman would also later declare that supporters had indicated 'in unmistakable Lancashire fashion' their own belief that the game was crooked. Enoch West's contribution to the game came under the spotlight in the *Daily Dispatch*, whose reporter, 'Veteran', called him 'slow and ponderous' and suggested that he was 'chiefly

employed in the second half in kicking the ball as far out of play as he
could.' The most popular national paper of the day, the *Daily Mirror*
('certified circulation larger than any other picture paper in the
world') carried the match result but no report. This was also the case
in the *Sporting Life*. The *Manchester Football Chronicle* carried a
report of the game half way down its broadsheet front page on 3 April
under the heading, 'A Surprising Display' by reporter 'Wanderer':

> Yesterday's match at Old Trafford provided a fairly good first
> half, but proceedings after the interval were dull, tame,
> unenthusiastic and generally most disappointing. Neither team
> showed any real energy after the United had gained a lead of
> two goals and the football in the concluding stages was the
> poorest seen on the ground this season.
> Some of the comments I heard were very strong but quite
> justifiable. One famous old player said, 'You don't need the
> War to stop the game, football of this sort will do it soon
> enough.' Personally I was surprised and disgusted at the
> spectacle the second half presented. Hodge, Spratt, Anderson
> and Montgomery were the best men on the United side.
> Anderson scored both goals and his first was a beautiful shot.
> The opening was cleverly made for him by Montgomery who
> in the first half was the cleverest middle-man on the field.
> Spratt gave a splendid display and was the strongest back on
> view. He often beat Sheldon in masterly style. O'Connell
> missed a penalty but did a lot of good work and Norton was a
> big improvement on Wall at outside left.

Elsewhere in the same edition, the *Chronicle* carried war reports
– '4 Submarines Destroyed'; 'Enemy Aeroplane Set On Fire';
'Warfare at the Somme' – all more important in the scheme of
things, perhaps, than a suspect football match. Another view of the
game appeared in the *Liverpool Daily Post* (ten pages for 1d) in its
late edition:

> The weather at the outset was wretched but brightened up after
> the first quarter of an hour. The United attacked from the

opening and Scott made wonderful saves from Anderson, twice, and West. Very little had been seen of the Liverpool forwards. Although their play in midfield was good, their shooting was wretched, as can be judged by the fact that Beale had not to handle for over half an hour.

A more one-sided first half would be hard to witness. The Manchester forwards peppered the Liverpool custodian unmercifully although it was not until five minutes from the interval that their persistency was rewarded. Anderson, receiving the ball from the right, drove it into the corner of the net well out of Scott's reach. The second period opened in Manchester's favour and within three minutes they were given a penalty for hands, against Pursell. O'Connell's shot went ridiculously wide. Play evened out a little after this.

Manchester's defence, however, had not to extend themselves. Manchester's second goal came thirty minutes after the interval. A tussle took place in front of Scott, and Anderson netted from a ruck of players. For the winners, the outstanding players were Anderson, Meredith and Norton in the forward line, and O'Connell, excepting his penalty miss, who was very sound.

Liverpool's best men were Scott, who was very hard-worked during the first half; Sheldon's centres were always dangerous and Spratt at times did not know what to do with him; Longworth proved himself to be a reliable back and broke up many dangerous attacks. Nicholl and Miller on the Liverpool right were very tricky but Pagnam was very poor indeed. M'Kinlay was a dour half back. The result was a favourable one from Manchester's point of view and they rightly deserved the whole of the points.

This review of the game was not as harshly critical as some of the other scathing reports that emerged, although that might have been because of the very early deadline the reporter would have had to meet. The *Manchester Daily Dispatch* carried its match report under a heading of 'Liverpool Beaten – Lifeless Football in Second Half':

It was a game which would scarcely send the most enthusiastic United supporter mad with delight. The second half was crammed with lifeless football. United were two up with 22 minutes to play and they seemed so content with their lead that they apparently never tried to increase it. Liverpool scarcely ever gave the impression that they would be likely to score.

Haywood found Sheldon a very hot customer to hold. The first incident of note in the first half, the first ten minutes of which was played in a most uncomfortable drizzle, was a narrow escape for the visitors' goal from a corner kick. Meredith placed this on the crossbar. Immediately afterwards, Montgomery, after some delightful footwork, placed a tremendous hot shot into Scott's hands. United pressed hotly for a time but finished badly. West, on one occasion, shooting very wide when well placed. In the next minute Norton hit the post at the left side of the keeper. Anderson dribbled finely before delivering a point blank shot. Scott could only push to the feet of West but the best the United forward could do was to shoot wide.

Anderson again got through to harass the goalkeeper after Scott had saved from Potts. It was such a near thing that Anderson claimed the ball had been over the line. The referee, however, ruled against him and United proceeded to take four corners in succession. It was astonishing how the Liverpool goal escaped. After forty minutes the United display was deservedly rewarded. Meredith had worried M'Kinlay and Purcell [sic] to such an extent that Manchester were able to put in a beautiful pass to Anderson and the centre forward, judging the situation to a nicety, scored with a cross shot which Scott never saw.

Liverpool had a look-in just before half time when United led 1–0. Immediately on the resumption, Anderson forced Scott to a great save, the goalkeeper putting the ball over the bar from a close range drive. In the next United attack Purcell handled in the penalty area but to the consternation of the crowd, O'Connell put the kick wide. In a quick return to the United goal Pagnam headed dangerously over. There

was a lot of give and take play after this but after 23 minutes
United became two goals up – O'Connell pushed the ball out
to Norton, the winger centred perfectly, Anderson, Potts and
the Liverpool goalkeeper went for the ball together, Scott got
there first but the best he could do was to repel the ball
against Anderson who immediately rushed it into the net. In
the closing stages interest went out of the game.

Perhaps the most significant phrase in this report is that United
'apparently never tried to increase' their two-goal lead. Did the
reporter, who also wrote, 'I have seen very little worse football
than that which was served up in the second half' have any
inkling that the game had been rigged? According to writer Iain
McCartney, other reports claimed that United manager, John
('Jack') Robson, 'was disgusted by the performance and had left
the ground before the final whistle'. Robson, who had succeeded
Ernest Mangnall, took over in 1914 and was the first to hold the
title 'manager'. His predecessors had been known as 'secretary'.

As we will see later on, it emerged subsequently that a furious
row had broken out in the dressing room at half time between the
plotters and other players, who were opposed to the match-fixing
plan. Some members of the team were so angry that they
threatened not to come out for the second half, and there was
even doubt as to whether the game could continue. As it
happened, the match resumed – but it seems that there were two
games being played out on the Old Trafford pitch that day. On the
one side there were the conspirators, trying to rig the 2–0
scoreline. On the other side were players who were trying to
prevent this happening.

However the match as a whole is viewed, the penalty miss is the
most mysterious aspect of the game. Why did O'Connell take the
kick when Anderson was the usual spot-kick man? Was it so that
O'Connell could ensure that that ball did not go in the net? If so,
and O'Connell was involved in the plot, why would he
deliberately miss when the score was only 1–0 and he was looking
for a 2–0 scoreline? On the other hand, why would he try to miss
if he were not involved in the conspiracy – even he if knew of the

plan and was determined to bring about a different scoreline? Perhaps this was not part of the plan and O'Connell simply miskicked the ball. Perhaps he was a wind-up merchant supreme.

For their next fixture, held the day afterwards, United visited Newcastle and were beaten 2–0. Athletic *News* reported, 'West seemed very slow on the ball. He could never raise a sharp burst and seemed to be limping about from the start.' This statement backed up West's subsequent claim that his lacklustre second-half display against Liverpool the previous day was caused by an injury he was carrying. West was missing from the United line-up (replaced by Sandy Turnbull) when the team entertained Middlesbrough a week later, but he returned to play in all three of their remaining matches – scoring in two of them. In the light of what would later emerge, an article that appeared in *Thomson's Weekly News* of 3 April 1915 under the by-line of one Billy Meredith was significant:

With a charming regard for themselves and the clubs, and a disregard for the interests of the paid players the ruling bodies have decided that – no matter whether some clubs wish to do so or not – no club shall pay any player during the summer. So that, if he can't get work and is not eligible for the army he can starve for all the Association and the League care. The club may not pay the player during summer, but he cannot leave the club next August without a transfer fee. They refuse to pay him, yet he is theirs, body and soul, to hold or to sell at their own price.

Hardly the words of a man on good terms with the profession from which he earned his living. Suspicions about the way the Good Friday game had been conducted soon began to circulate and were eventually reported by the *Sporting Chronicle* a week after the match had been played.

There is almost as much about this Manchester v Liverpool match as there was about the Liverpool v Chelsea match of a year or two ago. Of course, some people may be unduly suspicious in the Spring, but unsavoury comments are made, and the repetition of these observations, if not checked, is not likely to do the game any good, when football needs every friend that can be found.

The *Sporting Chronicle* was referring to the match held on 13 March 1913 that had prompted an inquiry. Liverpool's team for that game had included Ephraim Longworth – the first man from the club to captain England – and Donald McKinlay. Further rumblings of discontent were heard, as in the 10 April 1915 edition of the *Manchester Football Chronicle* when 'Wanderer', referred to the 'wretched exhibition given on the Old Trafford ground – nothing could be calculated to do more harm to the game or the clubs'. The affair really became a major talking point, though, when the *Sporting Chronicle* carried a notice on behalf of a bookmaker calling himself 'The Football King' and offering a reward for information about the match. This notice was also printed and distributed as a handbill:

We have solid grounds for believing that a certain First League match played in Manchester during Easter weekend was 'squared', the home club being permitted to win by a certain score. Further, we have information that several of the players of both teams invested substantial sums on naming the correct score of this match with our firm and others. Such being the case, we wish to inform all our clients and the football public generally that we are withholding payment on those correct score transactions, also that we are causing searching investigations to be made with the object of punishing the instigators of this reprehensible conspiracy. With this object in view, we are anxious to receive reliable information bearing on the subject and we will willingly pay the substantial reward named above (£50) to anyone giving information which will lead to punishment of the offenders.

'Wanderer' in the *Manchester Football Chronicle* considered the plight of the club on 17 April:

If the club does go down the present team would not be at all likely to regain the senior division. My own opinion is that of recent seasons there has been far too much talk about money at Old Trafford and too little about football. It is prosperity which has caused the decline. The Manchester United players have been treated magnificently by the club. They have been given benefits of handsome guarantees when the club was really not in a position to wisely do anything of the kind. From all I can gather the golden time of the player has gone.

What a pity 'Wanderer' cannot return to see the plight of 'the player' today! The correspondent also warned, 'People are still talking about that wretched Good Friday match – and the rumours one hears are most unpleasant to people having regard for the club.' He called for an inquiry.

The season ended dramatically, with Everton winning the title by just one point from Oldham – who lost it in their final match, when they were beaten by – Liverpool. Within three weeks of the Good Friday game the Football League had set up a Commission to investigate 'certain complaints'. The Commission made it known that it would be interested in liaising with 'The Football King': 'We can readily understand the serious unwillingness of bookmakers to be robbed by a conspiracy on the part of players and we are just as determined that League football should not be degraded, disgraced and ruined by such reprehensible practices.'

The Commission consisted of Messrs H Keys, John Lewis (a former referee and a regular contributor to *Athletic News*), and Charles Sutcliffe, another former referee who, it would later transpire, was also a solicitor who worked for Manchester United – which may suggest a certain conflict of interests. The Commission gave an interim report to the Football League Management Committee in late April 1915:

We have made very careful inquiries and full investigation into certain rumours that an important League match played recently had been squared, but in view of the facts hereinafter set forth we are withholding any report at present. A football coupon issued last week has been brought to our notice containing the following announcement…[at this point they repeated 'The Football King' statement]. The allegations referred to are not made in connection with any particular match, and may refer to either of two. We can readily understand the serious unwillingness of bookmakers to be robbed by a conspiracy on the part of players, and we are just as determined that League football shall not be degraded, disgraced and ruined by such reprehensible practices as those referred to in the coupon under notice.

If, as is stated therein, direct bets have been made by players, such conduct is contrary to the rules of the FA, and in accordance with declarations by the FA and the Football League any such player found guilty would be put out of football for ever. The conspiracy alleged is a criminal offence upon which the aggrieved parties can take action. If the injured parties are not prepared so to act and will furnish us with any information justifying such allegations, or either of them, we are prepared to pursue our inquiries to the utmost and fearlessly impose adequate punishment, and anyone willing to supply any information should communicate with the Secretary of the Football League, T Charnley, Castle Chambers, Market Place, Preston, at once.

There is one further alternative. If the party responsible for the issue of the coupon referred to will publicly state the match referred to, and furnish us with his name and address, thus accepting responsibility for the publication of such coupon, the 22 players concerned will immediately take action for libel, and test the whole question in the Courts before Judge and jury. If this challenge is not accepted within fourteen days we shall know what construction to place on the anonymous allegations and shall issue a further report based upon our investigations.

This was a remarkable interim report. Were the Commission members giving an anonymous allegation too much credence? Were they trying to stay at arm's length so that (in the event that

'The Football King' failed to respond) they could sweep the whole affair under the carpet? Had they not heard any rumours from other sources? Did they allow the trail to go cold while wasting time on a document which was never sourced nor reliably validated (in much the same way that the pursuers of the Yorkshire Ripper were wrong-footed by the so-called 'Ripper Tapes' that ultimately proved worthless and misleading)? Did they feel they could not implement investigations of their own? And if so, did they give any consideration to the thought of bringing in the police to conduct an inquiry – and if not, why not?

It is not difficult to understand why 'The Football King' – even if genuine – was not tempted out into the open by this offer. And, as for the odds of 'the 22 players concerned' deciding to go to law to clear their names – well, betting without Knocker, you could have had 66–1 against with me! The Commission investigation would primarily have been concerned with a possible breach of the FA's Rule 42. This stated:

> An officer of an Association or club, referee, linesman or player shall not bet on any football match, and Associations and clubs are also required to prevent betting and the use of objectionable language. An officer of an Association or club, referee, linesman or player proved to have taken part in coupon football betting shall be permanently suspended from taking any part in football or football management.

Manchester United managed to gain just enough points from their remaining games to stay in Division One. Following their defeat against Newcastle, they lost 5–0 at Bradford Park Avenue two days later and then 1–0 at Oldham on the following Tuesday, thus dropping to the bottom of the table. But they managed to beat fellow candidates for relegation, Chelsea, 5–1 on 20 April and ended their campaign with a 1–0 victory over Aston Villa, which lifted them just above the drop zone. At the end of the 1914–15 season, the English Football League Division One table looked like this:

Team	Played	Won	Drawn	Lost	For–Against	Points
Everton	38	19	8	11	76–47	46
Oldham	38	17	11	10	70–56	45
Blackburn	38	18	7	13	83–61	43
Burnley	38	18	7	13	61–47	43
Man City	38	15	13	10	49–39	43
Sheffield United	38	15	13	10	49–41	43
Sheffield Weds.	38	15	13	10	61–54	43
Sunderland	38	18	5	15	81–72	41
Bradford PA	38	17	7	14	69–65	41
Bradford City	38	13	14	11	55–49	40
West Brom. Albion	38	15	10	13	49–43	40
Middlesbrough	38	13	12	13	62–74	38
Aston Villa	38	13	11	14	62–72	37
Liverpool	38	14	9	15	65–75	37
Newcastle	38	11	10	17	46–48	32
Notts County	38	9	13	16	41–57	31
Bolton	38	11	8	19	68–84	30
Manchester United	38	9	12	17	46–62	30
Chelsea	38	8	13	17	51–65	29
Tottenham	38	8	12	18	57–90	28

These were to be the last League Division One games played until the Armistice. When war had broken out in 1914, the Football authorities, anticipating an early end to hostilities, had decided to continue the new season as usual. But as team members enlisted in the services and the clubs' ranks became depleted, so the appetite of the public for the sport also began to decline. On 20 April, partly in response to increasing pressure from politicians and others – and the fact that gates at matches had dropped off significantly – the FA announced that, following the completion of the 1914–15 season, professional football would cease until the end of the war. Frederick Wall of the FA told the *Sporting Chronicle*, 'There will be no more association football cup ties or league matches next season.'

Instead of national leagues, there were to be localised football competitions – known as Wartime Regional Leagues – which many of the professional players would take part in. With the season at an end, players were beginning to disperse. Some, such as Sheldon, signed up for the army, while United's Anderson, O'Connell and West had all gone into war supplies jobs at the Ford Motor Works in nearby Trafford Park. The majority of Manchester United players were now no longer being paid by the club.

Meanwhile, the Commission was continuing its investigations and had questioned Jackie Sheldon of Liverpool and United's keeper Robert Beale, as well as Arthur Whalley – who had not actually played in the match. Other players were interviewed shortly before the FA Cup Final, which was played at Old Trafford on 24 April. 'Wanderer' reported in that day's *Manchester Chronicle*, 'Yesterday was a big day in Manchester. A Commission appointed by the Football League met at the Grand Hotel and although there was a deal of ridiculous attempted secrecy about it, it was chiefly concerning the Manchester United versus Liverpool match on Good Friday.' 'Wanderer' added that United's season had been disappointing and among the reasons he gave were 'a noticeable falling off of the speed and effectiveness of both Meredith and West'.

On 26 April, *Athletic News* reported on the Commission's investigation under the heading, 'Either a Fraud or a Libel' – 'The League have been investigating the ugly rumours that have been prevalent in Manchester concerning the Manchester United–Liverpool match. This match, it has been suggested, was arranged.' *Athletic News* referred to the bookmaker document as 'a football coupon' issued by 'The 'Football Kings'. Discussing what had been happening, 'A N' said, 'This report does not by any means disclose the very searching inquiries which have and are being made into the conduct of the game, and incidents connected therewith.'

The *Athletic News* of 3 May described Manchester United's financial position as 'one of real anxiety for the Directors'. The publication added that, 'a large sum of money has been expended in medical and surgical treatment for A Whalley, an injured player' and explained further that 'a number of players have obtained employment at a neighbouring motor works, and there are several who have agreements until 16 April, including Anderson, Travers and West'. It is not entirely clear from this whether the writer means that they have agreements with Manchester United, or with the Motor Works until that date. It would seem more likely that it means the agreement is with the football club as it is difficult to see how they would have been aware of personal arrangements made with the Ford Motor Company.

The Commission convened an official meeting, which took place at Manchester's Grand Hotel on 10 May. Unlike today, when the steady leaking of information to the media is an inevitable aspect of high-profile cases, the Commission managed to keep its affairs and investigations secure. There were just the occasional rumours that indicated that the inquiry was covering a wide swathe of the country. This might have been because the members of the two teams were now so widely dispersed, or because bets had been placed in many locations.

Commission members continued to question and interview those they believed had something to add to their deliberations, but they had still to make a public statement confirming which match they were investigating. *Athletic News* began to lose patience with the Commission's slow progress, stating on 31 May:

Hitherto we have honoured the rule of law by totally declining to discuss the matter. But public interest is intense and relentless. Rumours, and much more than rumours, have poured into this office since Easter, and it has only been by the exercise of great restraint that we have refrained from writing anything which might be regarded as prejudicing either side of an unsavoury case. From communications from our various correspondents the only fear we have is that [the commission's] inquiries will be unduly prolonged.

On June 7 *Athletic News* reported, 'The minutes of the last meeting of the Football League Management Committee make no reference to discussions of the alleged betting conspiracy by a few well-known players. The fact is, the commission have not yet finished their labours. There is a probability of players other than those of the clubs most concerned being involved in this affair.' Nothing further had been heard from the Football King or Kings (both forms of the name appeared in different source material), it revealed. On 9 August *Athletic News* explained that the commission was 'compelled to interview men who had no interest in football – save that of exploiting it for the sake of speculation. Bookmakers have given valuable evidence and much circumstantial evidence has also been obtained. We understand that the whole of the information collected has been placed before the FA. If there are black sheep in the flock it is necessary to remove them'. On 23 August *Athletic News* carried an intriguing letter from someone signing himself 'Spectator' from Sale, who said he had been at the Good Friday match:

> I had no idea that this match would assume such importance in the football world, and the result [be] so widely discussed and questioned, especially by the betting fraternity. I was a close observer and my opinion is that the match was not squared, but that United adapted themselves better than Liverpool to the wet conditions. In the second half there was one incident I should like to point out when Anderson kicked the ball over the goal-line into the net at the Old Trafford end and, after the ball had crossed the line Longworth scooped it out with his left foot. Why did the referee disallow this goal for which Anderson strongly appealed and pointed to the mark made by Longworth's boot in scooping the ball out? If United players wanted 2–0 why did Anderson claim the third goal which he scored and which was disallowed?

This letter has the hallmarks of a poorly constructed attempt to defend the plotters. The only mention of this scenario I have discovered appears in a *Manchester Daily Dispatch* report of the game which is detailed and written in chronological style. This report states that the incident happened in the first half while the score was 0–0, so it would have been quite acceptable for Anderson to claim a goal at that point as it would have fitted in with the agreed outcome. Perhaps, also, Anderson was quick-wittedly making it appear as though he was trying to claim a goal while knowing full well that referees – as today – seldom change a decision once made. I believe this missive was a crude effort at backing up the accused players.

By September the Wartime Regional Leagues were up and running, with Manchester United and Liverpool both contesting the Lancashire

Section Principal Tournament. West was missing from the side initially, and the rumour mill started working overtime, but, writing in the *Manchester Football News*, 'H P R' put the record straight:

> There has been much wild talk as to the non-appearance of Enoch West in the side. I think it is only fair to the ex-Notts man to state that he has been keenly looking forward to taking his place in the team and did not fail to express himself when he found that he was not included – West, of course, has everything to gain by his active participation in the game, for he is a player with an agreement which also means a benefit match.

West was soon back in the team, scoring his first goals of the season in the third match, a 3–5 defeat at Bolton in which Knocker netted twice. A local newspaper report revealed that Billy Meredith, a man 'never really without a grievance', had yet to be paid 'the balance of his benefit money' by Manchester United. On 20 September rapidly growing public impatience received a voice when *Athletic News* declared, 'The failure of the Commission to deliver its verdict is enough to try the patience of Job.'

On 9 October, in the absence of O'Connell, Enoch West took over the captaincy of Manchester United (would Club officials have permitted this if they had reason to believe him guilty of nefarious behaviour?) when they travelled to Burnley and were walloped 7–3 – eight of the goals being scored within 42 minutes. During the afternoon a collection was made 'with the object of sending football tackle to the troops at the front'. Thus far, it was reported, United had sent sixty footballs to the soldiers. On 16 October, readers of the *Football News* learned that 'Sheldon is still taking part in football. The ex-Liverpool and Manchester United player had the honour of assisting the Footballers' Battalion last week under the command of Captain Buckley.'

'There has been a re-opening of the inquiry,' *Athletic News* told their readers on 18 October:

> On July 19 the Commission presented a final report to The League. Since then someone has slumbered ... it must

be inferred that there is reason for the latest move. Messrs J C Clegg; C Crump; D B Woolfall; J Lewis; H Keys and C E Sutcliffe, sat for three hours in Manchester on Friday and have adjourned for a week. For an hour they deliberated before any player was called in, then Woodcock, Lowe, Beale, West and Howard (Manchester City) were examined in turn.

This is the first account in which an 'outside' player – Fred Howard – was mentioned by name, and it emerged that 'near the end of last season Fred Howard (Man City) was suspended by his club for a breach of discipline. The suspension was reported to the Football League, who confirmed it and instructed the club that the suspension must not be removed without the consent of the League'. That must have been a serious offence.

Manchester's Mosley Hotel hosted another Commission meeting, 'A N' reported on 25 October, when Liverpool's Sheldon and United's Turnbull were quizzed. West was reportedly a very close friend of Turnbull. 'A N' added that, 'other players were expected but did not appear'. On 23 October, the *Football Chronicle* reported on Manchester United's 3–0 win over Stockport. 'West's form seems to be falling off. He missed chances and did not have much energy in the second half.' The *Manchester Chronicle* ran a front page article on 30 October that revealed a belated and scarcely credible request by the Commission:

It seems to be very late in the day for the FA to be asking for the names of the players who participated in the match between Manchester United and Liverpool last Good Friday, which has been the subject of inquiry by two Commissions. But I understand the clubs have recently been asked to supply the teams that took part in the game. It is to be hoped that nothing has gone wrong with the records or the files at Russell Square, but if the controlling body of the game have not this most necessary information after all the hubbub and inquiry that has been going on for seven months past, the followers of the pastime who have awaited the result of the investigation with such interest are hardly likely to have more than a hazy idea for the central figures in this momentous matter, at all events not when the decision is given, whenever that may be.

On 30 October 1915 Manchester United beat Liverpool 2–0 at Anfield. Enoch West netted the first goal – which would also be the last he would score for the club. Only Scott, Longworth, McKinlay and Pagnam from the Good Friday side were still turning out for Liverpool, although Lacey, who had been left out that day in favour of Fairfoul, was in the team. Only O'Connell and West survived for Manchester United. Knocker earned an unflattering review from the *Manchester Chronicle:* 'West was a failure as visiting centre forward – quite out of form and lacked pace.' 'Wanderer', too, was considering Enoch West's form in that game. On 6 November he wrote:

It was rather strange that West should score so brilliant a goal thirteen minutes from time at Anfield because all the game he had been slow and weak at centre forward. No man can get a finer goal than the big fellow from Hucknall Torkard, and this was a fierce, sudden and characteristic effort. I have seen him get fine goals. I remember a particularly brilliant one against Notts County at Old Trafford a season or two ago. This effort at Anfield was one of the brightest and best.

The Commission's plodding investigation continued. In early November *Athletics News* grumbled, 'A state secret was never so jealously guarded' while grudgingly accepting that 'we should be grateful to those who are probing the mystery to its depths.' On 15 November *Athletic News* divulged, 'After an interval of three weeks the commission held another meeting in Liverpool last Friday. All the Liverpool players, except two, who played in the game attended. The great offence is a charge that a conspiracy existed for the purpose of robbing bookmakers.' This was a new revelation. 'The commission must either be able to say guilty without hesitating or the players ought to be freed from the suspicion which attaches to every one of the 22 men.' There was much speculation in the press about the outcome of the investigation. 'J R C' of the *Manchester*

Football News stated, 'I gather that the outcome will be a verdict of "not proven".' He went on:

> I have seen it stated that what lent colour to the belief of an arrangement was the rush to back the actual score in places as widespread as Newcastle and Nottingham. I know that money poured into several centres and that bookmakers were badly hit in Manchester. But it is suggested that this was a mere coincidence. At all events it has been found impossible to prove that there was between the players anything in the nature of an arrangement.

The Commission worked slowly and patiently – unfeasibly so, thought some. 'It would appear that the Commission had been appointed for the period of the war' was one critical newspaper observation. On 20 November Manchester United travelled to Blackpool for a match but 'at the last moment West was dropped' reported the *Football News*. Whether there was any wider significance in this move, other than simple team selection based on his recent form, is not clear. On 27 November 'Wanderer' in the *Manchester Chronicle* now announced a serious turn of events. Having reported optimistically, 'It may be presumed that the joint commission of the FA and Football League has now completed its investigations,' he went on:

> It seemed to be expected in some quarters that the report and findings would be issued yesterday when they sat for several hours until nearly 9 p.m. at the Grand Hotel in Manchester – and received further evidence from a number of players. Probably because it was considered better that the result should be announced through the usual channel from Headquarters, no statement was issued to the press. From conversations I had with several of the players who gave evidence, there is reason to believe the inquiry has taken a very serious turn. It has been stated, I believe, and with some pretence to authority that the whole thing would end in smoke and that no suspensions would follow – that the indictment would be found not proven. That is not my information.

'J R C' had now changed his tune. 'There is every probability of the investigation ending in a much more definite finding,' he warned. On 29 November 1915 *Athletics News* announced news of the progress of the inquiry and on the same page carried an article noting, 'We are told of clubs making huge profits and growing dissatisfaction amongst players.' The *News* also reported that the Commission now included C Crump; D B Woolfall; H Keys; J Lewis; C E Sutcliffe.

The commission had yet another – and final – session. Before them at the Grand Hotel, Manchester, on Friday last were Meredith, Turnbull, O'Connell, West, Anderson, Woodcock (Manchester United); Howard (Man City) and Messrs H Hardman and J J Bentley, representing Manchester United officials – their attendance does not suggest any charge against the club. We anticipate findings within a week's time after which we shall be free to write what we know.

By 4 December, when the Commission had still failed to make an announcement, the *Manchester Chronicle* correspondent 'Volant' was musing:

Wherever you go you will find the hanger-on, the men who cultivate the acquaintance of the players and not always for the latter's good. Such limpets should not be encouraged and certainly not to the extent of admission to the dressing rooms. The players' quarters should be strictly private to all but players and officials. A strong dose of German gas would be required to move some of the individuals that are met with on almost every ground and who seem to regard it as a sort of right to walk into the referee's room.

'Volant' seems to be hinting that some shady middle men had played a part in the affair. On the same day the *Manchester Football News* was reporting on Manchester United's goalless draw at home to Southport Central the previous week and bemoaning the absence of West from the line-up. 'Had he been in the side last weekend one point instead of two [surely the other way round? – GS] would have been guaranteed at the expense of Southport. A man with the weight and resoluteness of West was just the individual required.'

On 6 December *Athletic News* predicted that the findings would be out 'in a few days' and also carried an article claiming that some players were reportedly receiving 'boot-money' payments and/or 'extravagant expenses' for turning out for clubs. Two weeks later, on 18 December, 'Volant' asked plaintively, 'What can have gone wrong with the report of the Commissioners? Something unforeseen must have happened to cause the delay. The FA and Football League have not hurried the inquiry. They have spared neither time, trouble nor money to get at the truth.' 'Volant' had less than a week to wait for enlightenment.

7

The Verdict

The Commission investigating the Good Friday match issued their long-awaited final verdict on 23 December 1915. Their findings were reported on the back page of the Christmas Eve edition of the *Sporting Chronicle*, under the heading 'Football Betting Commission Report – Eight Players Permanently Suspended – Manchester United v Liverpool, 2 April 1915':

The Commission appointed first by the Football League, and afterwards by the Football Association, have fully investigated the rumours and allegations largely circulated in several districts during and immediately after the above match, to the effect that the result was pre-arranged for the purpose of betting and winning money thereby. A mass of information was received.

The allegation of squaring the match carried with it a charge of conspiracy by some of the players, and as a result of long and searching investigations we are satisfied that a number of them were party to an arrangement to do so, and joined together to obtain money by betting on the actual result of the match.

It is proved that a considerable sum of money changed hands by betting on the match, and that some of the players profited thereby. Every opportunity has been given to the players to tell the truth, but although they were warned that we were in possession of the facts some have persistently refused to do so, thus revealing a conspiracy to keep back the truth. It is almost incredible that players dependent on the game for their livelihood should have resorted to such base tactics. By their action they have sought to undermine the whole fabric of the game and discredit its honesty and fairness.

We are bound to view such offences in a serious light. The honesty and uprightness of the game must be preserved at all costs, and although we sympathise greatly with the clubs, who are bound to suffer seriously, we feel we have no alternative but to impose the punishments which the players have been warned over and over again would be imposed. We are satisfied that the allegations have been proved against the following:

J Sheldon, R R Purcell, T Miller and T Fairfoul (Liverpool). A Turnbull, A Whalley and E J West (Manchester United), L Cook (Chester), and they are therefore permanently suspended from taking part in football or football management, and shall not be allowed to enter any football ground in future. There are grave suspicions that others are also involved, but as the penalty is severe we have restricted our findings to those as to whose offence there is no reasonable doubt.

F Howard (Manchester City) is suspended until the expiration of twelve months after the registration of professional players has been resumed by the Football Association, for the unsatisfactory and contradictory manner in which he gave evidence before the Commission. There has never been the slightest allegation against the clubs or their officials. It is therefore unnecessary to exonerate them from blame or complicity, and we are indebted to them for much assistance in our investigations.

This Report was presented to the Emergency Committee of the FA, which recorded it in the 'Minutes of the Proceedings from 13 July 1915 to 31 December 1915', but made no additional comment about the findings.

The *Liverpool Echo*'s football correspondent, 'Bee', feared it to be 'the worst blow football has had'. He declared, 'The governors of football have never, and will never, countenance betting on football.' Nor would he accept any pleas of mitigation from the guilty parties. 'The excuse, if such it can be called, has been made that players were tempted into the sordid business through the belief that the war would prevent football in 1915–16 and summer wages would be the rule. It is too paltry a claim and can be ignored.' 'Bee' continued his rant in the Christmas Eve edition of the newspaper:

The smell from the stigma cast upon football will permeate the air for many a day. The punishment of the players was severe. It was deserved. Whalley's inclusion in the list was a surprise packet. Sheldon's cost to Liverpool was expensive – his transfer fee was in the region of £1,000, therefore his club have lost that sum. There are some lucky fellows connected with the inquiry, that's certain. It is a fact that some fellows have scraped through the inquiry 'by the lip of their mouth'.

This last comment suggests 'Bee' believed that more Liverpool players were directly involved. If so, he clearly had good contacts at the club who had been feeding him this information. The *Echo* disclosed another interesting snippet, 'The Commission even went to certain theatricals who had shown an interest in football affairs and they travelled to the extreme north and south and studied points of value in the midlands and Staffordshire.' The *London Daily Chronicle* opined, 'This habit of betting on football matches is not very popular in the south but for some years there has been a big market in the midlands and the north. The FA and Chief Constables have done their best to kill the evil.'

Under the heading 'Big Football Sensation', the Christmas Eve edition of the *Sporting Life* announced, 'The penalty is indeed severe, but FA rules themselves prescribe the punishment if players or officers are proved guilty of betting on the game.' Also on Christmas Eve, the *Liverpool Daily Post and Mercury* reported that Sheldon 'is now at the Front with the Footballers' Battalion,' and that Miller, 'is in a Scottish Regiment at the moment.' They said of Whalley, 'injuries kept him in the background last season.' This was something of an understatement. In fact, he played just one game all season for United because of a damaged knee. The newspaper described Howard as 'a strong, dashing player, leader of the Manchester City attack'. The *Post* added, 'From Liverpool's point of view it is good to see that a section of the club has cleared itself before the commissioners.' This was putting a positive spin on what many might have regarded as a disgrace.

The Manchester-based *Daily Dispatch* commented, 'There are certain things in an inquiry like this that even yet need to be rooted out. The Commission has not yet told us everything we would like to know.' In fact, the Commission had offered very little hard proof to justify convicting the eight players named. The *Daily Dispatch* also boasted an interview with John McKenna – chairman of the Football League and a director of Liverpool Football Club. McKenna told the newspaper:

> I created the Commission which sat upon the case and so long as the party was found guilty of an offence there could be but one decision – they had to be ousted from the game of football. We could not have football coming down to the level of other sports that are mixed up with betting, such as pedestrianism. The warning-off notice refused the men permission to go to a football ground – this has been done so that there shall be no contamination. My position as Liverpool director made matters a trifle awkward.

In another interview in the *Daily Dispatch*, McKenna said : 'I am sorry that the other players who were engaged in the match did not assert their individual views at the time and stamp out the foul plot.'

There seemed to be some confusion regarding both the identity and role of Cook. The *Liverpool Echo* noted, 'Confusion arose in our minds when the name Cook was included. William Cook is the long-time Oldham back, but Lol Cook played for Stockport County and never for Oldham.' That confusion continues to this day.

The 'plight' of the bookmakers and the motives of the plotters were examined by *Athletics News* on 27 December under the heading 'The Manchester United–Liverpool Match, Permanent Suspension of Celebrated Players.' Below this was the sub-heading 'Robbery!'

> We have great sympathy with some of those who will have to live under a cloud in that they participated in this hippodrome

hocus-pocus and this nefarious contrivance to rob bookmakers who had no chance of preserving their own property. We have not a scrap of compassion for those who have been punished for, not only devising the result of the 'match' but for taking money from the pockets of bookmakers, who are as much entitled to the protection of the law as other men. Some people do not approve of their business, but the majority of them are at least as honourable in their payments as those engaged in ordinary trading. Indeed, had it not been for the bookmakers, who corroborated [sic] in a most emphatic and extraordinary manner, the collusion between the culprits in the rival camps could not have been proved. There was a carefully worked out plan by which the bookmakers in whole districts were filched at such odds as seven and eight to one against the actual result. Places so far apart as Liverpool, Manchester, Nottingham and London came within the sphere of operations. In one or two instances the suspicion of the bookmaker was aroused by the actual result and the amount of money tendered. Generally speaking, the bookmakers paid their clients although they discovered that they had been 'rooked' but a few refused to disgorge. That is not our business.

What Was the Temptation?

It may be urged that these footballers succumbed to temptation because of the reductions in wages that they had suffered and because there was no probability of any salaries during the summer months as have been customary. This cannot be justly urged in mitigation of their crime for many other people have lost their earning capacity during this war, but they have not lost their honesty. Presumably these men connived to 'make a bit' so that they would not feel the pinch of poverty. There must have been some personal motive. We do not believe that there was any cause for their action other than personal aggrandisement. Does not this exposure indirectly suggest the wisdom of insisting upon a law that the man who plays football for money must at the same time work for his livelihood? Wages from football should be supplementary and not the sole support of any man. It is quite probable that had these players been engaged in skilled handicrafts or even in situations where trained eyes and hands are not essential they would not have succumbed to this temptation. They saw their income disappearing, and had ample time to work out their deep-laid designs. That, however, is merely a consideration, and is not even a palliation of their diabolical machinations. The money they have handled will pollute their lives, for they have enriched themselves in a manner which not only disgusts the public and defrauds bookmakers, but threatens the very existence of the game to which hundreds of other professionals have honestly devoted themselves for legitimate and, in scores of cases, ambitious and honourable purposes.

Power Justly Used

But there are aspects, even of this affair, which should assure the public. The decision of the joint commission of the League and FA proves that those who govern the game are determined that the spectacular sport as presented by professionals shall be honest and pure. Rather let the whole fabric, so laboriously built up, collapse like a house of cards than that such venal practices should be permitted. The moment that rumours were reported to the President of the League, he appointed a commission to investigate. There was no hesitation even though his own club was concerned. The commissioners scoured the country for information. They forwarded the result of their minute searchings in all kinds of nooks and corners to the FA who then came on the scene. Taking no imputation for fact the association joined hands. There came a time when there was a deadlock. The authorities were convinced that the match was unreal but that the offence could be brought home to one man only. At this juncture there was a sudden revelation from one quarter, and proof was piled on proof. The authorities were impartial. They did not screen their eyes or stop their ears. They have punished drastically. Said a great writer, 'Justice discards party, friendship, kindred.'

Simon Inglis surmised that the 'sudden revelation' referred to must have been an insider squealing, possibly 'one of the players finally cracking under the strain of deceit'. So who was the 'one man only'? It could surely not have been Knocker. His name apparently appeared, disappeared and reappeared on the Commission's list of 'possibly' and 'definitely' guilty men as they deliberated. Perhaps it was Jackie Sheldon, or could the 'revelation' have perhaps come from the enigmatic Lol Cook whose role in the entire affair remains shrouded in mystery to this day? *Athletic News*, commenting on Cook's part in the scandal, mused, 'Lawrence Cook's complicity with Whalley and Turnbull presumably rests on their share of the ill-gotten gain and the part they took in the scheme.'

Athletic News expressed some sympathy for the bookmakers who had lost out to the scam, declaring that the majority of such folk conducted an honourable business. One wonders how much sympathy there would be for 'layers' if a similar scam took place today, but then perhaps I have just become jaundiced after thirty years of seeing matters from a bookie point of view. Another article in the same edition of *Athletic News* was headed 'The Grave Scandal':

A plot to cheat the public, to sell to the faithful followers of football a sham instead of the genuine article, to rob book-makers by criminal fraud, and to conspire for the suppression of the truth has been revealed. For the moment the game of Association football, as played by professionals, staggers under the grave scandal that the League match between Manchester United and Liverpool last spring was a complete and deliberate fake. Hitherto any irregularities proved have been in the main offences against the rules and regulations of football, but this alleged contest amounts to a breach of the criminal law of England. It is not an offence to bet, but it is a crime to make wagers and obtain money by false pretence.

In its 17 April 1915 edition, the *Manchester Football Chronicle* noted that 'half a dozen of the Old Trafford players have secured employment at the large Ford Motor Works situated near the ground'. Enoch West was now employed there as a mechanic. This was regarded as a reserved occupation – 'war work' – and so he had not been required to join up, despite having applied to the forces. His protestations of innocence were no doubt greeted with some scepticism by his work-mates, at least initially, especially those who had previously been his team-mates.

The *Sporting Chronicle* commented on the case on 29 December 1915 in an article entitled 'The Football Scandal: Some Reflections on the Recent Trouble'. This appeared alongside an article reporting that three footballers – Tim Coleman of Nottingham Forest and England; G MacDonald of Norwich and R Dalrymple of Portsmouth and Fulham had been killed in action. The *Chronicle* announced:

It has been proved that this actual result was arranged – those men converted what should have been a genuine contest into a circus performance. Nine men have lost their livelihood – one of them [West] has forfeited a benefit which was guaranteed under an agreement. No words can too strongly condemn the base conduct of professionals who enter into such a conspiracy – the game will be the better for the absence of those men who did not yield to a sudden temptation but met in Manchester, carefully planned their coup and carried it out in spite of opposition.

It is passing strange, nay incomprehensible how only one man of the Manchester United XI has been found guilty. There must be others. Sympathy on E J West would be wasted, but it does not seem right that he should bear all the burden of this infamy and that his accomplices, because he must have had them, should be free. There has never been anything like it before and with such drastic measures already taken there will, I venture to think, never be a repetition. I have every reason for believing that there was a quarrel in the dressing room of the Liverpool team when one half of the men confessed what they had done – there was a strong section in favour of an honest game.

The matters reached such a pitch that the real footballers refused to play – the honest group only consented to waive their objections when it was realised that there was a huge crowd round the arena and that if there was no match there would possibly be a riot. The difficulty of the rogues was to keep the ball away from the honest men when they were so placed as to be likely to affect the result. Let us remember that J McKenna appointed a Commission to inquire into the conduct of players of his own club.

Howard of Manchester City was alleged to have made money by betting on the result – this he denied. Some allegations were made against other professionals – they all deny that they ever had a bet at all. I fail to see why West should bear the whole burden for the birds of prey in the United camp.

This extraordinary article put forward the bizarre notion that the Manchester United v Liverpool contest actually consisted of two games – not only that between the two sparring clubs but also between the honest players and the conspirators. It isn't clear exactly when the honest players found out about the plot – before the match or at half time – but the *Chronicle* article conjures up an image of one set of players trying to keep the ball away from other players on their own side. This was an unprecedented situation in which one set of players – on both sides – were trying to engineer a 2–0 scoreline while the others were trying to decide whether to react passively, simply refusing to co-operate in any way, or to actively endeavour to ensure that the 2–0 scoreline did not come about. Whatever, the missed penalty incident assumes an even greater significance. Did O'Connell know about the conspiracy or not? And if so, what was he trying to achieve by missing? At this stage none of the accused made a public declaration of their innocence – or at least, none that had been reported.

Both Enoch West and Fred Howard had been expected to play for their respective clubs in the United–City derby on Christmas Day 1915. Both were dropped. Sandy Turnbull and Arthur Whalley were due to play for the Second Football Battalion against Birmingham, but were not permitted to do so. In the same week, Manchester United had announced a loss of £3,732 4s 8½d for 1914–15 – having made a profit of £1,937 6s 9d in the previous season. The club directors also announced that seventeen of their players – including eight who had appeared in that season's team – had joined the Forces. After crunching the figures, *Athletic News* mused:

Possibly the enlistment of some of them provided a happy solution of a difficult situation. In glancing at the accounts of Manchester United we notice that the wages of players in 1913–14 were £5,573 15s and in 1914–15 £5,810 1s 11d. There does not appear such a reduction here as should tempt any man to scheme for money in an illegitimate manner. The football which the United team showed last winter was not worth £112 per week. The players had bonuses of £60, and the travelling expenses cost £909. The receipts of the first team matches declined from £13,397 to £6,081, and the total revenue fell from £16,022 to £11,708. The debit balance is not surprising when the players take £5,810 out of £6,081 taken at the more important matches.

Simon Inglis concluded, 'All this, added to the fact that men like West would have been about to receive lucrative benefits, made the illegitimate attempt to make a few extra pounds on Good Friday appear even more loathsome.' But, is this a fair picture? It is not as though West and his colleagues were earning wages on a par with the Beckhams and Van Nistelrooys of today. And was it their fault that Manchester United were losing money? There could have been any number of reasons for the club's parlous financial state. This was an era of consistently large crowds. The modest wages paid to the players were unlikely to have been a significant factor. And with West due for a benefit match that would have made him hundreds, if not a couple of thousand, of pounds, just why would he put it at risk for a profit on a bent game?

The footballing authorities played the incident down and declared: 'When we consider that League football has been a vogue for 26 years, the number of matches that have aroused suspicion is extremely small. We have no hesitation in saying that 99 out of every hundred games are honest contests'. Perhaps mathematics was not the Football League's strong point, but that statistic, if taken at face value, was suggesting that there was at least one suspect First Division game being held every ten weeks – that is four dodgy games per season.

Manchester United were quick to distance themselves from their disgraced players. The *Manchester Football Chronicle* reported on

1 January 1916, 'The directors accepted the blow dealt by the Commission in the philosophic spirit and plainly declared their opinion that the suspended men had received only what was fully deserved and necessary for the good of the game.' On the same date, the *Manchester Football News* said that Howard 'was not concerned in the conspiracy by which bookmakers were defrauded of many hundreds of pounds' and suggested that he 'seems to have been merely foolish and not vicious'. The newspaper continued:

Why did these players descend to such knavery? It was simply because a few men saw the end of all things when it was announced that there would be no summer wages. The plot was conceived and entered into so clumsily and so recklessly that half Football England rang the same day with the news that the match had been faked and the bookmakers fleeced. The whole plan of campaign smacked of the gambling novice. I say without hesitation that such a wholesale plundering had never previously been attempted and would not have taken place had there been no war and no stoppage of wages.

In its 3 January 1916 edition, *Athletic News* suggested that it was generally known that, through lack of evidence, not all of the guilty players had been punished:

We hear that one of the players concerned is taking advice and threatening legal proceedings. Another player is also talking a great deal. We should like to know the names of those among whom no suspicion rested. We see that one player has admitted the justice of the report and declared that all the guilty have not been punished. No one need tell the Commission that fact. They know it.

There was another tricky problem for the football authorities to consider. The outcome of the United–Liverpool game had ensured that Manchester United would avoid relegation, leap-frogging Chelsea, who went down to Division Two. On 7 January 1916 the Football League confirmed that the result of the match would stand.

A Management Committee Meeting adopted the resolution, 'In view of the difficulties of the circumstances, the match was ordered to stand as a League match.'

At this juncture, what else could they have done? But *Athletic News* had a suggestion, 'Either the game must stand, or be replayed. There are strong arguments in favour of both contentions. We should like to see the game replayed.' Almost unbelievably, Chelsea did not immediately object to the FA's decision to uphold the result. Chairman of the club's directors, W Claude Kirby, said, 'Chelsea support the decision of the Football League Management Committee that the result stand as recorded, in the most sporting spirit possible.'

It is difficult to envisage Ken Bates or Roman Abramovich wholeheartedly endorsing such an announcement without registering even the slightest doubt. In fact Chelsea would belatedly reconsider their statement and protest the FA's decision. *Athletic News* certainly had misgivings. It commented, 'Manchester United have been extremely fortunate in escaping from the consequences of the acts of men for whom they are technically responsible.' The *News* added, mysteriously, 'The United players have for years caused much trouble. The forbearance of the FA some years ago and the beneficent neutrality of the League has saved the club. Manchester United enjoy a place they have not honestly won and Chelsea are called upon to suffer an indignity they do not honestly deserve.'

'H P R', writing in the *Manchester Football News* of 8 January 1916, blithely asserted, 'It is hard luck on Chelsea, but United would probably have won the game in any case. There certainly appears to be some individuals who would like to see the Old Trafford club swept off the face of the earth.' Surely not?(!) In the same month, George Anderson left to play for Belfast United. This dismayed Manchester United, who held his registration, and the club immediately suspended him *sine die*. Anderson's suspension was lifted in October 1916, but only when he returned from Ireland to resume playing for United.

The unlikely sympathy for the bookies expressed by several newspapers did not last long. In the 15 January 1916 edition of the *Manchester Football Chronicle*, columnist 'Volant' reported on rumours of 'another squared match with the object of swindling the bookmakers.' 'Volant' dismissed the allegation, writing, 'I don't believe it for a moment. I regard it as idle and mischievous rumour with no other foundation... unless it may be that it has had its genesis in the cowardly squeal of some broken bookmaker who has been deservedly hoist by his own petard.'

So, already the gratitude to bookies who had, according to many, been responsible for blowing the whistle on skulduggery, was being replaced by claims that bookies were acting purely out of self-interest. 'Volant' demanded, 'What is to prevent any unscrupulous backer from setting up the cry that he has been "rooked" when the book has gone against him?'

'Volant' also touched on the question of whether blame should attach to the clubs involved. He commented, 'While Manchester United and Liverpool were exonerated from all blame, I cannot help but think that in the capacity of employers they were to some extent responsible for the acts of their servants. Clubs can and must be expected to have in their service men whom they can trust.'

There was general incredulity that only one member of the United team on the field that day had been singled out (the other two United players listed had not been in the side). As Simon Inglis queried, 'Surely Knocker West could not have rigged the game for United on his own?' According to *Athletic News*, 'Here was the weakest point in the Commission's report'. Although the *News* declared that 'the public must assume that the others who played are all honest men', it struck a cautionary note:

In one sense we must say that we are puzzled. How comes it that so many players are let off? There is only one Manchester United player [in the team that day] suspended. It is beyond the power of human credibility to assume that only one of the eleven players was 'in the know'. We can only assume that the Commission had their 'grave suspicions' but failed to find such clear proof as would warrant the severe punishment which would naturally follow. The truth will out, and we are satisfied we have not even yet heard the last of this unsavoury business.

Jackie Sheldon had gone off to War but, despite having to worry about whether he would survive the conflict, he was still preoccupied by the outcome of the Commission's report. While he could have spent his time writing to his loved ones at home he sat down to write to *Athletic News*, who published this fascinating missive on 10 April 1916 under the heading, 'Private J Sheldon of the 1st Football Battalion (17th Middlesex) writes from "somewhere in France" in relation to the notorious match':

> Would you kindly give me space in your valuable paper to explain my position re suspension? Perhaps it is unfair for me to ask this favour. But you will understand how difficult it is for me to explain while doing my bit somewhere in France. I am now taking the first opportunity I have had and wish to let the numerous followers of football know how I stand. I emphatically state to you, as our best and fairest critic, that I am absolutely blameless in this scandal and am still open, as I have always been, to give to any Red Cross Fund or any other charitable institution the sum of £20 if the FA or anyone else can bring forward any bookmaker or any other person with whom I have had a bet. Assuming I return safely from this country I intend taking action against my suspension and in the meantime you would do me a great favour if you would kindly insert this letter in your next week's issue.

On 22 April 1916, almost as though they were already seeking to welcome him back to the fold, the *MFN* published an article by correspondent 'J R C' under the heading, 'Wiping Out The Stain':

> Even though it was alleged that John Sheldon (before he was so unexpectedly transferred to Liverpool) had been guilty among others of striking the deadliest blow imaginable at the game by means of which he earned his livelihood, I am sure that a good deal of sympathy will go out to him now that he is lying in hospital. Sheldon made a belated protestation of his innocence and whether or not he was justly put out of football is now a matter of no great account for he has done much to

wipe out the stain on his name. [Presumably a reference to his service in France since joining the Footballers' Battalion] He is now in hospital at Aberdeen. As an operation has been performed it was assumed that he had been wounded but I learn that the trouble arose from a loose cartilage of the knee.

Why had the Commission failed to produce in public one bookmaker who would be prepared to state the name of those suspended players who had definitely placed a bet on the game? In my experience bookmakers are never backward in coming forward if they believe they have been duped.

Enoch West was certainly not prepared to admit to any guilt. He festered away, wondering how to prove his innocence. Simon Inglis wrote, 'West was so angry that, against the advice of his solicitors and at great personal cost, he went to extraordinary lengths over the next four years to clear his name.' It is not clear how the former player would have funded this quest. Cynics might suggest he had won enough from his match fixing exploits, but there is no evidence I can discover to support such a theory.

On 18 March 1916 (and/or 7 October 1916) – it is not quite clear which one it was, or maybe both – West, who lived very close to the Old Trafford ground, in Railway Road, joined the crowd heading for a Lancashire Section Principal Tournament match (the wartime regional substitute competition) between Manchester United and Liverpool. He was carrying leaflets clearly designed to ape 'The Football King' handbills that had helped spark the Commission's inquiry. Like 'The Football King', West also offered a £50 reward, to be donated to charity, to anyone who could prove that he had placed a bet on the outcome of the rigged match. As West was banned from entering the ground, he stood outside handing out the leaflets. The games both ended in a goalless draw – not that Enoch would have cared. His plea was not taken up. West's offer of a payment to charity if anyone could produce proof that he had placed a bet was remarkably similar to the challenge Sheldon had made in the newspaper – perhaps the two had been corresponding.

On 3 May 1917 Sandy Turnbull, one of the suspended players – banned despite taking no part in the match, was killed in action in

France. He was initially reported as 'missing believed wounded' and possibly 'picked up by the Germans'. In June, Mrs Turnbull still believed that her husband was being held prisoner in Germany. The news must have upset Enoch West – but it certainly did nothing to lessen his desire to continue the fight to prove his innocence. On 5 July 1917 reportedly against the advice of his solicitor, West went to court to claim damages for libel against both the FA and E Hulton & Co Ltd – the latter as publishers of the *Sporting Chronicle* and the *Daily Dispatch* over articles that had appeared in those newspapers. He was also calling for his ban to be overturned. West appeared before Mr Justice Ridley and a 'special jury'. The *Daily Dispatch* reported:

> The hearing was begun of an action in which Enoch James West, professional footballer of Railway Road, Old Trafford, Manchester, claims damages for alleged libel against the FA Limited and Messrs E Hulton & Co Ltd. Plaintiff also asks for an injunction restraining the FA from putting into force a resolution suspending him from taking part in football or football management. Messrs Hulton admitted publication of certain statements about the plaintiff's conduct as a football player, but pleaded justification and fair comment.
>
> Opening the case, Cyril Atkinson KC for West, said that Enoch was now engaged in the Ford Works at Manchester, but had previously been engaged by Manchester United for three years receiving £4 10s a week for one year and £5 per week for two, the club undertaking also to give him a benefit which should amount to £500. The rules of the FA, said Counsel, forbade players to bet on football or enter football competitions, throwing the onus on the player to prove he was not guilty of any charge.

Note that the principle of 'innocent until proven guilty' appeared to have been dispensed with here. It was explained that the Commission's first meeting, held at Manchester's Grand Hotel on 10 May 1915, had heard West deny any knowledge of the rumours circulating that strongly suggested that the game was not entirely honest. Other players had also been interviewed. Knocker attended another Commission meeting on 15 October, this time at the Mosley Hotel in Manchester. Now he was asked about a letter he was alleged to have written to a Mr Clarke in Hucknall Torkard. The Commission said it had a copy of this letter in its possession. West declared that no such missive existed. [Crucially, I can find no record of it ever having been produced or displayed. To support the Commission's implication that the letter incriminated Knocker, why did they not simply show it? – GS]. West had left Hucknall Torkard eight years previously, he said. He had not made a bet on the match. He had done his best in the match. He added that until he was questioned by the Commission he had no knowledge 'that he was suspected of taking part in a conspiracy'.

The court heard that West attended a third Commission meeting on 26 November, at the Grand Hotel. Once again West denied any involvement in or knowledge of the whole affair. He said that Sheldon had not told him on the Monday before that the game was to be squared with a 2–0 result. West said that he was never asked directly by the Commission whether he was involved. He added that following his ban he had attempted, on legal advice, to seek a hearing before the FA but the FA would not permit it. West claimed he had asked for this as he had seen the Commission's record of the evidence he had given them and that it contained nothing detrimental or incriminating about him. West alleged, 'They convicted me without hearing me and I don't think that is fair.'

Asked about public reaction to his performance during the game, West replied, 'A football player gets criticised more than any man living.' This raised laughter in the court. O'Connell, too, appeared before the Commission and told them that he 'had nothing to do with any squaring, and it had never been suggested'.

Mr Atkinson, representing West, suggested that there had been 'a tossing up' by the Commission as to which players to name and which not to name. Jury members should ask themselves, said Mr Atkinson, whether West was a party to match-fixing; whether he had swindled a bookmaker; whether he had actually placed a bet on the outcome of the game; whether he had deliberately played for a pre-ordained result.

Turning to the match itself, West explained that he had played up front in the first half, only to be told by his skipper, O'Connell, to drop back in the second half, during which he was suffering pain from his bandaged ankles. Mr Atkinson told the court, that despite this West 'played the proper defensive game having regard to the critical position of his club'. According to a report of the case in *The Times*, West said he had been told to 'play safe', which meant 'hugging the ball'.

Cross-examined by Mr Rawlinson KC, MP, representing the FA, West was asked, 'Did you on Thursday, 1 April, see Anderson, your centre forward, whom I am going to call, and tell him that you had written to Nottingham to get £10 put on the match ending 2–0 at odds of 7–1, and did you add 'They won't get any evidence against me?'

'No,' answered West.

'Did you think the match was squared?'

'Not to my knowledge'.

'What do you think?'

'Well, the papers made such a show of it, it makes one think. I don't know what to think. If people admit that the match was squared, I can't think any other.'

'Were the crowd shouting at you "Play the game"?'

'I do not know,' replied West, 'I never take any notice of what the crowds say. If a player takes notice of them it causes him to lose his grip of the game.'

However, West did admit that he thought it was odd that heavy betting on the game had been reported from Hucknall Torkard, his own birthplace, and where he still had relatives.

Patrick O'Connell, the player who had missed the penalty during the game and who was now a foreman at the same factory at which West worked, now appeared in the witness box. O'Connell said that he was unaware of any attempt to 'square' the game and testified that West had produced his usual performance during the game. When asked about the missed penalty O'Connell commented, 'I have missed dozens in my time', which does rather make one wonder why he had been permitted to take the penalty in question.

Other witnesses – J Winston, a cotton merchant, J M Turnbull, a former professional and now a munitions worker, and Albert Raffo, a publican, all testified that they considered that there had been nothing out of the ordinary about West's play that day. Raffo said it seemed that there had been a great deal of betting on the match. According to the *Dispatch*, Raffo claimed to have heard bookmakers say 'it had been squared'. Raffo said he had seen three or four bookmakers in the grandstand and from what they had said 'he thought they intended to indicate that the match had been squared and that the result would have been 2–0'.

Liverpool winger Jackie Sheldon, evidently back from 'somewhere in France', was now retracting his claim, made in a letter published in *Athletic News*, that he was 'blameless in this scandal'. He told the court that he *had* fixed the game with players from his own side. He also alleged that he had met West, Turnbull and Arthur Whalley, in a Manchester pub – The Dog and Partridge – where they had agreed on a 2–0 outcome, with one goal either side of half time. Sheldon said that several players were aware that the match had been rigged and had placed bets. However, he did absolve Billy Meredith, one of the most controversial yet charismatic players of his era, from any involvement in the plot.

How can we explain Sheldon's apparent about-turn? His letter from France to 'A N' denied that he had placed any bets on the match and the evidence he now gave did not contradict that. But if his testimony was to be believed he was hardly 'blameless'. His inconsistent claims and denials must raise reasonable doubts over his assertion that West knew of the pre-ordained outcome of the match.

George Anderson, now working as a 'cotton manufacturer', also appeared and repeated the claim that West had placed a £10 bet. Anderson said that he had met West and two others at the Great Central Station in Manchester, the day before the match when he had discovered the plot. They had then repaired to a small pub at the back of the Prince's Theatre. Anderson having previously denied all knowledge of a fix now said he had been offered £3 to take part. However, he refused to join in. Sheldon had told him to keep quiet about it and Anderson had agreed. Anderson claimed that West had won £70 by betting on the score and had boasted, 'I am not afraid. They cannot get any evidence against me.' Anderson said he had changed the story he had told the court because 'I was tired of telling so many lies', a remark that prompted laughter in court. He said he had considered refusing to play in the match but had done so because he might otherwise have scuppered his team-mates' plan.

He also said, 'If I had been able, I should have scored another goal, but I was never given a chance.' 'Did you have a bet?' he was asked. 'No'.

Liverpool centre forward Fred Pagnam, now in the Royal Garrison Artillery, whose shot had hit the woodwork, said he had learned of the scam from Sheldon, while in a taxi *en route* to the match. Sheldon told him that each player would get £3. Pagnam said he would not do it for that sum, which also caused some hilarity in the court. Pagnam had not been pleased and had threatened to 'bang one in', only to be warned that he would be 'bloody well finished' at the club if he did so. Despite the threat, Pagnam said he went out and tried his best anyway.

Ephraim Longworth and Donald McKinlay of Liverpool both appeared and stressed that they had been aware of the fix but had not co-operated. Indeed Longworth said he had warned his team mates at half time to keep the game straight, while McKinlay claimed he had been told to 'lie down' by Sheldon but had refused.

Robert Pursell of Liverpool had gone along with the scheme and had telegraphed to a friend in London to put a £1 bet on the outcome at odds of 6–1, planning to take half of the meagre winnings for himself. 'Do you agree that the betting was robbing bookmakers?' Pursell was asked. 'Yes'.

Referee John Sharpe, who by now was a sergeant in the army, called it 'the most extraordinary match I have ever officiated in'. He claimed that O'Connell's penalty had obviously been played deliberately wide. Linesman Fred Hargreaves agreed. Sharpe also said that in the second half 'West kicked the ball to the top of the grandstand instead of towards the goal'. [Sharpe was to survive the War and resumed his refereeing career at the top level in the 1919–20 season.] United boss John Robson confirmed that he, too, had felt the game was crooked. Robson, extraordinarily, even claimed to have confronted West after the match, asking him why he had kicked the ball out of play so often, only to be told, 'What would you do if you had a number of matches to play in a few days?'

Billy Meredith said that he only became aware that something was going on when the game was underway. The other players were deliberately keeping the ball away from him. Meredith had asked Robert Beale, the goalkeeper, whether he was aware of a fix, but Beale said that all he knew was that Sheldon had told him he was in for a quiet afternoon.

Anderson contradicted Meredith's assertion that he had not known what was afoot before the game. Asked by Mr Atkinson KC, 'Do you say Meredith was not playing fair?' Anderson said, 'I think that they all knew something about it before.' But Meredith insisted that he did not know about it until the game began. He was asked, 'In your opinion, could anyone have played in that game without suspecting there was something wrong?'

'No.'

'Was there any reason for such play [keeping the ball away from him] at a time like that?'

'No.'

'If you had got the ball were you perfectly fit and ready to go on and take advantage of it?'

'Quite.'

Meredith's biographer, John Harding, says that the veteran had been 'disgusted by the whole affair', but adds 'Meredith's part in this shabby business seems to have been a peripheral one. Perhaps he watched the furtive arrangements going on from the corner of the dressing room and simply turned a blind eye – he had seen it all before, and suffered the consequences. Perhaps he no longer cared what went on among his colleagues. He was forty years old; the majority of his playing colleagues were half his age.'

Yes, but such was his standing in the game that it is impossible to believe that the conspirators would have even attempted to organise something of this nature if they felt there was the slightest chance he may blow their cover. Meredith had himself been suspended for eighteen months for attempting to bribe Aston Villa's skipper – 'though he protested his innocence vehemently, there can be little doubt that he was central to a conspiracy to pervert both the course of a game and the destiny of a championship.'

And Harding's revelation that 'Meredith never spoke again about the betting ring scandal; he would simply laugh, shift his toothpick from one side of his mouth to the other, and change the subject' paints a picture of a man who knew more than he was prepared to divulge.

Part-time bookmaker E Giles, who also worked as a 'moulder', said that the volume of bets he had been offered on the game had made him suspicious and that he had lost £150, although he had turned down enough business to have given him a potential loss of £1,500. The odds for a 2–0 scoreline, which would usually have been 8–1, had shortened as low as 4–1. 'All the bets were the same. I began to think something was wrong.' This is a typical bookie reaction, as I can testify, after thirty years working among the breed. But bookies are not always right. Sometimes a story does the rounds that a certain outcome is pre-ordained, causing a bandwagon effect and a rush to back the same team, country or result.

FA Commission member – and former international referee – Charles Sutcliffe now appeared. He gave his opinion that West had given contradictory evidence to the Commission and was definitely prominent in the affair, although he wouldn't accuse him of placing a bet. Sutcliffe added, 'Inquiries among bookmakers showed the state of things mentioned by Giles was prevalent.' He testified that West had admitted to being present at the Dog and Partridge when the plot was hatched. 'There must be two sides to the squaring of a match,' Sutcliffe said, and he had 'set himself to look for those in the Manchester United team who were concerned.' In his opinion, 'West stood out from the rest.'

It had been admitted by Sheldon and other players that West was with them at the Dog and Partridge on the Monday before the match. West made statements 'which he afterwards contradicted'. The crowd at the match had 'particularly selected West' and he – Sutcliffe – 'had evidence of members of the press'. He did not suggest that West had put money on the match, but bookmakers had told him that they had taken bets from West's friends. Mr Atkinson, on behalf of West, said that at first the Commission decided not to implicate West, 'but there was evidence on which the jury might find that they altered their mind from the fear of appearing ridiculous by declaring the match squared but implicating nobody.'

A point well made. It certainly took the Commission long enough to come up with just one Manchester United player that day.

Justice Ridley pointed out that when the Commission first tried to report it had chosen not to implicate West but had they not implicated anyone from United 'not only would the commission have looked ridiculous but it would also have been guilty of malice.' Yet Ridley seems not to have considered that by implicating West ultimately they were certainly malicious towards him.

Justice Ridley said that the only question for the jury was 'the complicity or otherwise of the plaintiff'. The Judge said that he had assumed that the match had been squared in a manner which was 'a shame and a disgrace to this country, especially that part where it occurred', but he then added that 'the complicity of West had not been proved by the verdict of the jury, but it had been found by the Committee of the Association.' The Judge ruled that West had not been libelled and that the FA ban should remain. John Harding, who has written a history of the Professional Footballers' Association, is scathing about this verdict:

> The Judge ruled for the FA and Hulton Newspapers. The rules of natural justice, he decided, need not apply in cases decided upon by the FA, because the latter was a privileged institution, with a duty to prevent dishonesty in the game. As long as the FA acted without malice, then those bound to obey its rules – i.e. clubs and players – must accept its judgements whether they feel they have had a chance to defend themselves or not. The professional footballer, it seemed, was still outside the law; the FA was still his lord and master.

As if to back up Harding's unsympathetic view of the football authorities, an Ordinary General Meeting of the Shareholders of the Football League Limited was held at Manchester's Grand Hotel, on Monday, 16 July 1917, at which League president John McKenna stood up to review the League's year's work. Referring to the recent West action, he said that no one was more delighted than he at the result of the case, and at the endorsement of the decision and finding of the Commission which he, connected with one of the clubs concerned, appointed to investigate the matter as soon as it arose.

> It was the first extraordinary attempt made to 'square' a match and rob the public and bookmakers, for even bookmakers had a right to be regarded as honest except where they were found to be otherwise. There was no honesty in it beyond any cavil or doubt, and it was gratifying to those gentlemen who had spent so much time in investigating it, and to Messrs Hulton & Co, who had attacked the abuse of the game in manly fashion that their attitude had been upheld by the High Court.

This pious outpouring showed a hypocritical streak in McKenna which would reveal itself in word and deed before long.

West was soon called into the forces, and became a driver in Ulster. He attempted to play football under the alias 'Reeve' but failed. Ever persistent, West appeared at the Court of Appeal on 11 February 1918, seeking to overturn the verdict. His representative, Mr Atkinson, contended that, 'it was not enough that the plaintiff should merely be informed that he was under suspicion. He must be told what the substantive charge against him was. He should have had an opportunity of contesting and contradicting the statement made against him.'

Mr Rawlinson, for the FA, said, 'The onus was on the plaintiff to prove that the proceedings at the inquiry were not conducted in accordance with the principles of natural justice,' adding, 'the court ought to be very careful before it interfered with the findings of a private tribunal.'

The Judges dismissed West's appeal against the FA and Hulton & Co, 'except on one point, on which a new trial was ordered.' Lord Pickford 'was of the opinion that there was evidence of a matter which was capable of bearing a discriminatory meaning, which ought to have been left to the jury, and there must be a new trial on that point.' The appeal against the FA was dismissed with costs, and a new trial ordered against Messrs Hulton & Co. The costs of the appeal and the costs of the first trial were set aside until the result of the new trial.

In March 1918, George Anderson – still only 26 – was charged by the police with 'having conspired with persons unknown who had made bets on the results of various matches'. Anderson denied the charges, but was found guilty and sentenced to eight months imprisonment with hard labour. Although no proof was produced that games had actually been fixed, seven professional players – including four from Manchester United – gave evidence that Anderson had offered them cash for helping to ensure certain results. It had been suggested in Court that Anderson may have been working for a large Scottish-based bookmaker. He denied this. However, Anderson did admit to running in a foot race under an assumed name – J Andrews – not uncommon in such events in those days. And not unheard of even today.

An item in the Minutes of Proceedings from 1 January to 31 March 1918 of the Emergency Committee of the Football Association recorded, 'It was unanimously decided that George Anderson be suspended from Football and not be allowed on Football Grounds in the future.' The item made reference to matches between Oldham and Blackburn; Manchester United v Burnley and Everton v Blackpool. The minutes also revealed, 'A meeting of the Joint Commission of the FA and the Football League was held at the Grand Hotel, Manchester on the 19th February 1918, when further evidence was heard, including George Anderson and his witnesses.' Anderson's conviction for match fixing must cast doubt on his own evidence against West. He may well have been looking to implicate West as a scapegoat and so draw attention away from his own dodgy dealings.

A curious item appeared in the minutes of the same Emergency Committee of the Football Association under the heading 'Manchester United v Liverpool – Letter from Mrs Turnbull with regard to the removal of the suspension of her husband, J Turnbull.' It was recorded that, 'The Secretary was instructed to express sympathy with Mrs Turnbull, and to inform her that applications of such a character could not be entertained at the present time.' This is truly strange. If this is a misprint and the J Turnbull referred to here was actually Sandy Turnbull, then he was already dead at the time, killed in action on 3 May 1917, and the FA were showing a gross lack of feeling in rebuffing a plea for mercy from his widow. If the name J Turnbull was accurate then it must refer to the former United striker Jimmy (no relation to Sandy – although they did play together) who had been replaced by Enoch West. Turnbull had returned to United from Chelsea, on a month's trial in September 1914, only for the Old Trafford management to decline the fee required by the London side – more evidence of how financially vulnerable they were at that time. But I have found no evidence to suggest that Jimmy Turnbull had been suspended.

Perhaps more pertinent to our story, those minutes also note that the Football Association sought a 'Bankruptcy Petition against Enoch James West, in respect of a Judgement recovered against him by the Association in the High Court of Justice on the 9 July 1917, for the sum of 11s 11d [just under 60p], which sum remained due and unpaid'. Clearly the FA were determined to pursue Knocker to financial oblivion regardless of the fact that there was a war on.

On 15 January 1919, a month after George Anderson was released from prison, the persistent West returned to court in yet another attempt to win libel damages against the FA and Hulton & Co. The case was before Justice Darling. In his case, West raised the question of the loss of his potential benefit earnings, which he put as high as £2,000. He alleged that Manchester United could have supported the allegations about him in order to avoid having to pay such a sum. West was now claiming that an *Athletic News* article in which he was described as 'Manchester United's solitary defaulter' represented unfair comment and, according to *The Times,* 'charged him with having been a party to a criminal conspiracy to defraud bookmakers by arranging the result of football matches and by betting on those matches.' This was the first – and, as far as I am aware, the only – time that more than one match had been implicated.

Extraordinarily, Commission member John Charles Clegg said that at their first meeting there had been little evidence against West and that there was a unanimous vote that he 'had no case against him'. He admitted, 'At the first meetings of the Commission West's name was struck out of the report.' According to *The Times,* the witness then said that West's name 'was restored to the report at a

Butter wouldn't melt? Not a hair
out of place in this formal portrait
of Knocker the neat.
(By kind permission of Eric West)

BELOW: Knocker never
shirked a fight in his life –
for real, or to brighten up a
training session. Here (right),
he squares up to a team-mate.
Would you mess with him?
(By kind permission of Eric West)

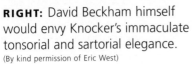

LEFT: Enoch West lived within kicking distance of Old Trafford. Here is his club house in Railway Road as it looked when this book was published. Note the view of the West Stand – no relation!
(Photographer: S J Rayner)

RIGHT: David Beckham himself would envy Knocker's immaculate tonsorial and sartorial elegance.
(By kind permission of Eric West)

OPPOSITE: The media furore that surrounded the revelations about the fixed match.

EN PASSANT.

THE GRAVE SCANDAL

A PLOT to cheat the public, to sell to the faithful followers of football a sham instead of the genuine article, to rob bookmakers by criminal fraud, and to conspire for the suppression of the truth has been revealed. For the moment the game of Association football, as played by professionals, staggers under the grave scandal that the League match between Manchester United and Liverpool last spring was a complete and deliberate fake. Hitherto any irregularities proved have been in the main offences against the rules and regulations of football, but this alleged contest amounts to a breach of the criminal law of England. It is not an offence to bet, but it is a crime to make wages and obtain money by false pretence.

Gentlemen of the Football Association and the League have investigated the circumstances of this match. They have been satisfied that there was a gross conspiracy which strikes at the fundamental basis of the structure of spectacular football.

The Findings of the Commission.

The report issued by the joint commission circulated by these governing authorities immediately follows :—

effect MANCHESTER UNITED v. LIVERPOOL.
APRIL 2, 1915.

The Commissions appointed first by the Football League, and afterwards by the Football Association, have fully investi-

The Manchester United-Liverpool "Match."
Permanent Suspension of Celebrated Players

Robbery!

We have great sympathy with some of those who will have to live under a cloud in that they participated in this hippodrome hocus-pocus and this nefarious contrivance to rob bookmakers who had no chance of preserving their own property.

We have not a scrap of compassion for those who have been punished for, not only devising the result of the "match," but for taking money from the pockets of bookmakers, who are as much entitled to the protection of the law as other men. Some people don't approve of their business, but the majority of them are at least as honourable in their payments as those engaged in ordinary trading.

Indeed, had it not been for the bookmakers, corroborated in a most emphatic and extraordinary manner, the collusion between the culprits in the rival camps could never have been proved.

There was a carefully worked out plan by which the bookmakers in whole districts were filched at such odds as seven and eight to one against the actual result.

What Was the Temptation ?

It may be urged that these footballers succumbed to temptation because of the reductions in wages that they had suffered and because there was no probability of any salaries during the summer months as have been customary. This cannot be justly urged in mitigation of their crime for many other people have lost their earning capacity during this war, but have not lost their honesty.

Presumably these men connived to "make a bit" so that they would not feel the pinch of poverty. There must have been some personal motive. We do believe that there was any cause for their action other than personal aggrandisement.

Does not this exposure indirectly show the wisdom of insisting upon a lay for the man who plays football for a livelihood must at the same time work for his hood? Wages from football should be supplementary and not the sole support of any man. It is quite probable that these players been engaged in situations handicrafts, or even in situations

Have We Heard the Last Word?

In one sense we must say that we are puzzled. How comes it that so many players are let off? There is only one Manchester United player suspended. It is beyond the power of human credibility to assume that only one of the eleven players was "in the know." We can only assume that the Commission had their "grave suspicions," but failed to find such clear proof as would warrant the severe punishment which would naturally follow.

If that is the case we do not complain, but there must be keen eyes and alert ears in the future, and it is the duty of every lover of the game who can furnish any evidence to do so. The Commission declares that there has been a conspiracy to keep back the truth

we are satisfied w
heard the last of th

Players must be
They must not be
stakes of knaves,
honest men, and
money in firm faith,
and a real game wi
are out for dishone
where. Permanent
effective remedy.
Commission have
truth, but it wor
greater pity if the
to find the truth
covered. Some ev
ad a wholesome c

Mr. M'Kenna's V

The decision of
great blow to the
which is deprived
arly half its first
cuniary point
crease in assets
terviewed on the
correspondent
Kenna, the pre
gue and vice-pr
ciation, spoke
ect.

I consider," s
ence is a just
are of the gam
tion of the
tigated

PLAYER'S SUSPENSION.

Claim for Damages and an Injunction.

PLAINTIFF'S DENIALS:

F.A. Allegations of "Squared" Match.

The hearing was begun in the King's Bench Division yesterday of an action in which Enoch James West, professional footballer, of Railway-road, Old Trafford, Manchester, claims damages for alleged libel against the Football Association, Limited, and Messrs. E. Hulton and Co., Ltd. Plaintiff also asks for an injunction restraining the Football Association from putting into force a resolution suspending him from taking part in football or football management.

Messrs. Hulton admitted publication of certain statements about plaintiff's conduct as a football player, but pleaded justification and fair comment.

Mr. Cyril Atkinson, K.C., and Mr. J. D. Crawford appeared for plaintiff, Mr. Rawlinson, K.C., M.P., and Mr. H. T. Waddy for the Football Association, and Mr. Rigby Swift, K.C., and Mr. B. Campion for Messrs. Hulton.

In opening the case, Mr. Atkinson said West, who was now engaged in the Ford Works, at Manchester, was playing for Manchester United until the end of 1915. He was engaged for three years, receiving £4 10s. a week for one year, and £5 a week for the last two years, the club undertaking also to give him a benefit which should amount to £500.

Playing the Safe Game.

The rules of the F.A., said counsel, forbade players to bet on football or enter football competitions, throwing the onus on the player to prove he was not guilty of any charge. West took part in a match between Manchester United and Liverpool on Good Friday, 1915. United scored a goal in each half, and then the team played what was called a "safe" game.

After the match rumours began to get about that the match had been squared. Bookmakers found that there were so many bets about the precise result that they suspected an arrangement and

ABOVE: Glossop 1934–5: Eric West (back row, second from left) and his team-mates. That year the team were the winners of the Derbyshire Divisional Cup and runners up in the Manchester League, Manchester Junior Cup and Gilchrist Cup.
(By kind permission of Eric West)

LEFT: Eric West. Knocker's son, still pugnacious at 93 when the book appeared but, smarting from his abandonment by his father at an early age, he remains to be convinced of his innocence.
(By kind permission of Eric West)

OPPOSITE: Official notice of a devastating snub to Knocker's hopes of reinstatement.

THE FOOTBALL ASSOCIATION.

MINUTES OF MEETING OF THE CONSULTATIVE COMMITTEE

Held at 42, RUSSELL SQUARE, LONDON, W.C., on MONDAY, 1st SEPTEMBER, 1919.

Present : Messrs. J. C. Clegg (in the Chair), C. Crump, W. Pickford, A. Davis, J. McKenna, J. Howcroft (Vice-Presidents), A. Kingscott (Hon. Treasurer), W. H. Bellamy, E. Case, A. J. Dickinson, M. C. Frowde, W. W. Heard, A. G. Hines, H. Keys, T. H. Kirkup, J. Lewis, R. E. Lythgoe, H. A. Porter, M. T. Roberts, G. W. Simmons, J. B. Skeggs, A. J. G. Stancomb, C. E. Sutcliffe, H. Walker, W. J. Wilson and F. J. Wall (Secretary).

1.—Minutes of Meeting of the Council of 2nd June, 1919, were confirmed.

2.—The Report of the Proceedings of the Emergency Committee from 27th May to 25th August, 1919, was received.

> Letter from the Players' Union asking the Council to reconsider the decision of the Emergency Committee refusing to remove the suspension of E. J. West, of Manchester United F.C. It was unanimously decided to decline to reconsider the application.

3.—The Minutes of the Annual General Meeting of the Association of 2nd June, 1919, were received.

4.—Finance.—The Finance Committee reported that the Receipts from 1st May, 1919, amounted to £510 11s. 5d., and the Payments to £836 2s. 5d.

5.—The Secretary reported the Election of the Divisional Representatives to the Council as follows :—

> Division 1.—H. Walker (North Riding County F.A.).
> 2.—C. E. Sutcliffe (Lancashire F.A.).
> 3.—Dr. J. C. Baxter (Everton F.C.).
> 4.—H. Keys (West Bromwich Albion F.C.).
> 5.—A. J. Dickinson (Sheffield Wednesday F.C.).
> 6.—W. T. Hancock (Nottingham Forest F.C.).
> 7.—J. B. Skeggs (Millwall F.C.).
> 9.—H. J. Huband (London F.A.).
> 10.—H. A. Porter (Kent County F.A.).

Division 8.—Candidates : Mr. J. G. Stone (Chesham United F.C.) and Mr. S. Bourne (Crystal Palace F.C.). The Election resulted in a Tie, each Candidate receiving 6 votes.

> [Rule 14 provides : " If there is a Tie the Election shall be determined by a vote of the Members present at the first Meeting of such Members of the Council as shall have been duly nominated."]

Mr. J. G. Stone (Chesham United F.C.) was re-elected.

ABOVE: Manchester United 1913–14. Back row: Hodge, Gipps, Knowles, Beale, Stacey, Hamill, Whalley. Front row: Meredith, Woodcock, Anderson, West (and close-up, right) and Wall. Flat caps, moustaches, wrap-around laces and plastered down hair cannot disguise the determination and folded-arm confidence of Enoch and his United colleagues.

20 Oxford Court, Bishopsgate
Manchester M2 3WQ

Telephone: 0161 236 0575
Facsimile: 0161 228 7229
Email: info@thepfa.co.uk
Website: www.givemefootball.com

PROFESSIONAL FOOTBALLERS' ASSOCIATION

Chief Executive: Gordon Taylor BSc (Econ), HonDArt, Hon MA

GTkjc 24

10th June 2002

Mr G Sharp
Media Relations Director
William Hill Organisation Ltd
Greenside House
50 Station Road
Wood Green
London N22 7TP

Dear Graham

Thank you for your letter of 28th May and your research regarding the game between Manchester United and Liverpool on Good Friday, 1915. I will look to see if we have any material referring to that game and the charges by the FA at that time, especially as you say, a number of the players were very prominent Union members.

I would also certainly be part of support for you to establish the innocence of Enoch West if the evidence is strongly in favour of this.

I will also refer to the PFA Historian on this matter and get back to you at a later date.

Yours sincerely

Gordon Taylor
Chief Executive

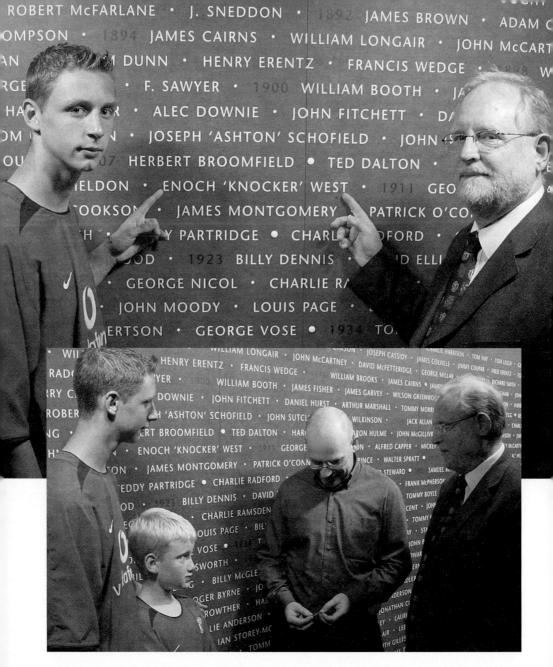

TOP: Across the generations: Roger West (grandson) with his own grandson, Daniel Chadwick, who is therefore Enoch's great-great grandson, pointing out the name of their infamous relative on the Manchester United Museum 'Wall of Honour'.

(Photographer: S J Rayner)

ABOVE: The United Museum curator, Mark Wylie, who was consistently helpful as this book was researched, examines Enoch's First Division Championship 1910–11 medal, as Roger West, his grandson, Daniel Chadwick, and his son, Thomas, eight, look on. (Photographer: S J Rayner)

later meeting after fuller discussion'. West's solicitor, Mr Atkinson stressed the fact that West's name had not been included in the first draft of the report.

West himself gave evidence in which he declared that 'according to the number of years I have played (for Manchester United) I ought to have received 50 per cent of my transfer fee', yet he 'obtained only £250 on the transfer' and thought that he ought to have had more, but he was not told what the transfer fee was. It was reported by the media as either £450 or £500 but, of course, it might have been more.

Simon Inglis has revealed that West, 'claimed that Manchester United had deliberately sanctioned the allegations against him in order to avoid paying out his benefit money. It was a wild charge, and fortunately for him not taken seriously.' But why 'fortunately'? Enoch may have been more sympathetically regarded had this element of his defence been pursued. *The Times* reported that the Good Friday match was 'within three months of the expiration of [West's] contract when he would have been entitled to a benefit. Some benefits amounted to as much as £2,000. He was aware of the penalties for betting, and he knew if he betted he would lose his benefit.'

In cross-examination by Mr Rigby Swift, West admitted that after the two United goals had been scored, he was 'kicking into touch – playing a safe game as an honest man'. West said he 'did not hear the crowd jeering and shouting for their money back.' He had never bet on a match, nor had he ever told anybody that he had had a bet on the match.

Football League Management Committee member Charles Sutcliffe appeared again, admitting that at one stage the Commission had actually removed West's name from the list of guilty players. He again accused West of giving contradictory evidence, notably that O'Connell had told West to drop back in the second half – which he said had been denied by the skipper himself. Sutcliffe said he had heard rumours about the game on the day it took place and that subsequent enquiries had taken place in Manchester, Liverpool, Nottingham, Derby, the Potteries, Newcastle, London and Glasgow – all visited by Commission members. They had spoken to bookies and found there had been large-scale betting on the result of the match – in every instance the wager was on a final scoreline of 2–0. In the Hucknall district, the people who had placed bets were reportedly members of West's family. One bookie had paid out £200; one £150; another £38. Of course this raises the issue of why shouldn't members of a famous player's family bet on his team winning a match without attracting suspicion?

The Commission had seen all the players involved in the game, as well as members of the press and spectators, and had asked them about the play and the betting. Sutcliffe said that all had singled out West's performance in the game, which he had claimed had been influenced by O'Connell's instructions. Sutcliffe said O'Connell was the last witness to be called before the Commission and had denied that he had ever asked West to 'fall back' and play defensively. Sutcliffe himself had prepared the first draft of the report, he said, and West's name was on it.

John Lewis, a member of the Committee of the FA and vice president of the Football League, said he was sure West's name should have been in the report. He said West had denied having relatives in Hucknall, had claimed to have no knowledge of any betting in that district, or that he had sent information about the match to anyone.

The Times reported that, 'The jury returned a verdict for the defendants and judgement was entered accordingly with costs.' West was beaten again, ironically enough, 2–0 in court. Where was the money coming from to pay for these cases? Did he have any money? Had the FA yet managed to force West to hand over the 11s 11d they said he had owed them. And had he been declared bankrupt? Answers to these questions remain elusive.

Athletic News, which had had a vested interest in the outcome of the case, reported the appeal under the heading 'Blots on the Game'. The newspaper said, 'The second hearing of the case brought by E J West against *Athletic News* and the *Sporting Chronicle* for libel, ended as before. On Friday a special jury took the same course, deciding that we had not exceeded fair comment in a matter of public interest.' Revelling in the verdict, the newspaper now went somewhat over the top:

The result of this suit has been to strengthen the hands of the FA for their rules, regulations and bye-laws have been found unassailable by the Court of Appeal while newspapers will be encouraged to express their opinions boldly when the sport of football is besmirched by players who should be the first to preserve it from any plots which tend to undermine public confidence in the genuine character of the play. So long as the FA deal justly with offenders they have nothing to fear from the law and so long as critics adhere to the truth and nothing but that they will discharge a duty of value to the community.

The *News* then gave the somewhat vague warning, 'We regret to say that we have not yet heard the last of football scandals as both in London and the Midlands there are again grave allegations which must be examined. At all costs the game must be preserved from wreckers.'

In January 1916 *Thomson's Weekly News* carried a story with the title 'Allegations of another Arranged Match in the south – What's the cause of it all?' The newspaper stated, 'The confounded betting evil! How many times do we hear men saying "Only for such a match I should have been well in this week." If I were to give an opinion at all I should say the whole thing should be taken with a pinch of salt. Players are not the fools that many folk credit them with.'

By February 1919 Chelsea had finally launched their bid for reinstatement to the First Division. The Football League Management Committee Meeting, held in Birmingham that month, and attended by the League president, McKenna, and Charles Sutcliffe, among others, was told:

On the application of the Chelsea Football Club for a consideration of their appeal against being relegated to the Second Division, it was Resolved: The match, Manchester United v Liverpool having been declared by a Commission after a full and searching investigation to have been squared, and such decision having been upheld by the Court of King's Bench and three Judges in the Court of Appeal, the Committee feel that it would be unjust that Chelsea should be relegated to the Second Division.

As it is, and always has been impossible to replay the squared match under satisfactory conditions, the Committee feel it would be equally unjust to relegate Manchester United to the Second Division, seeing that the management of the club were neither party nor assenters to the squaring of the match or cognisant of it.

Under the unfortunate circumstances which have arisen the Committee thereupon decide to call a Special General Meeting of the Clubs, to be held at the Grand Hotel, 19 March 1919 at 2.30 p.m., at which they will submit the following proposals:

1. That the Football League be extended to 44 Clubs – 22 in each Division… If the above proposal is not accepted, Mr John Lewis will propose that for the next season the League shall consist of 42 clubs, 22 in the First Division and 20 in the Second Division. The 22 Clubs to form the First Division for next season shall comprise the present 20 Clubs, Chelsea, and a club to be elected from the Second Division. At the end of next season Chelsea or Manchester United, whichever shall be lower in the League Table, the elected club and the two clubs at or nearest the bottom shall be relegated to the Second Division, and the top two clubs in the Division be promoted in accordance with rule.

Two clubs shall be elected for the Second Division for next season only. If either resolution be carried Chelsea will be automatically returned to the First Division. Any necessary election of clubs will take place at the meeting a fortnight today.

This was, on the face of it, quite a clever scheme, ostensibly designed to allow both Chelsea and United the chance to prove themselves over the course of a whole season in a scrap against each other to determine which of them should ultimately be relegated. A side effect of the 'fix' was that Arsenal were 'promoted' into the First Division when football resumed following the war, despite having finished only fifth in the last completed season. They replaced relegated Spurs, so the Gunners should perhaps acknowledge Knocker's role in their history. Chelsea finished third in the

22-strong First Division in 1919–20, with Manchester United twelfth. But guess what? United remained in the First Division for 1920–21 – which also boasted twenty-two clubs – being joined by Second Division winners Spurs and runners-up Huddersfield.

Manchester United, who had condemned the alleged match fixing, but had nonetheless benefited substantially as a result, do not seem to have offered to do the decent thing and sacrifice the two points they 'won' from the game and which ultimately kept them above the relegation positions.

On 2 June 1919, in what writer Stephen F Kelly has referred to as 'an act of magnanimity', the four banned Liverpool players were offered a chance to apologise for their behaviour, in recognition of their Army service, and seek to have their suspension lifted. The FA's Emergency Committee adopted a resolution proposed by the chairman:

> The Council of the FA desires to place on record its high appreciation of the great sacrifices and services of its members during the war, and its deep gratitude for the success which has been achieved. With a desire to recognise with thankfulness the Peace which is now in sight, the Association will favourably consider applications from players, officials and others connected with the game, for the removal of their suspensions. Applications relating to suspensions by County Associations should be made to the County Associations concerned.

All four Liverpool players applied, their bans were lifted and all except Fairfoul resumed their careers. Sheldon went on to play seventy more games for the club and was even granted a benefit match by Liverpool after breaking his leg in 1921. Miller went on to be capped for Scotland and in September 1920 was even transferred to – of all clubs – Manchester United. Pursell made only two more appearances for Liverpool's first eleven.

This was a surprising act of forgiveness by club supremo and Football League President John McKenna, who had been so scathing about them at the time the Commission had announced its verdict. McKenna, who had handed the club chairmanship over to

W R Williams in 1915, but remained at the helm, seemed to have forgotten his wholehearted condemnation of the players and was now prepared to forgive and forget.

On 27 December 1915, McKenna had told the *Daily Dispatch*, 'Personally I am sorry that the players, and particularly those connected with my own club, have been so callous as to bring this discredit on the game. I regret that the decision did not come earlier for we have been engaging men to appear in our team who had we known their connections with this affair would not have been afforded the slightest sympathy. We would have had no dealings with them in any shape.' Had he really meant that, or were these comments merely intended to impress the public and the media? What a difference a war makes. Oh, and perhaps the dawning realisation that the club was being deprived of the services of good players.

Manchester United's Arthur Whalley and City's Fred Howard were also permitted to resume their playing activities. Sandy Turnbull was automatically given a posthumous pardon after the FA Emergency Committee adopted a minute stating that, 'The suspension of all suspended persons formerly connected with the Game who have sacrificed their lives for their country shall be removed and the record expunged. The secretary shall on being informed of the address of the widow or near relative of any such person notify them of the pleasure of the Council in being able to remove the suspension and clear the record.' Ironically, as the 1919–20 season got underway, Billy Meredith was missing from Manchester United's opening line-up – he was 'in dispute with the club'. So, six of the banned players had had their suspensions lifted and one was posthumously pardoned.

Knocker also applied to have his suspension rescinded. But, as the FA Emergency Committee's minutes record, 'The application of E J West of Manchester United FC was refused.' Why? It could only be because he had dared – and continued to dare – to refuse to kow-tow to the football authorities and had been, until recently, engaged in a determined action to clear his name through the courts. What a shame Enoch hadn't gone off to war and been killed – they'd have pardoned him then! Petty spite was, in my opinion, the real reason that the FA was not prepared to forgive and forget. Their decision seems especially harsh when you consider that they had already decided to show mercy to Sheldon, who was generally believed to be the driving force behind the whole affair.

West now cut himself off from football entirely, but cast around for alternative ways of gaining support for his case. First he took his grievances to the Players' Union, who were evidently impressed by his persistence. They wrote to the FA asking the authorities to reconsider their decision. But with no success. On 1 September 1919 the FA's Consultative Committee 'unanimously decided to decline to reconsider the application.' Later that month, the Players' Union were congratulated by 'J R C' in the *Manchester Football News* for expressing 'their resolve to do all they can to counteract the evil' of coupon gambling on football. If this was the Union's attitude it seems unlikely that they would actively be supporting any player they genuinely believed to be guilty of an offence relating to betting on football.

West hit on another way of highlighting what he continued to insist was the injustice that had been done to him, launching a petition to try to drum up popular support for his case. West believed that the press were against him, and so he did not bother to alert the media to his latest plan. Instead, he had a circular printed that he distributed to factories and other businesses in the Manchester area. I have now discovered the wording of this document, which has languished forgotten or ignored for over eighty years. Under the heading 'An Appeal For Justice' the circular proclaimed:

> I appeal to all followers of football for their aid in endeavouring to remove the suspension from playing which I am now undergoing. Most people are aware of the circumstances under which several players and myself were suspended and, rightly or wrongly, I do not think it English justice that all the players concerned should have their suspensions removed while I should suffer alone. As you are aware, I have consistently appealed against the embargo against me and I earnestly appeal to all interested in football, in fact to all sportsmen, to extensively sign the petition which is being organised on my behalf for the removal of my suspension in common with the several other players who,

fortunately, have had theirs cancelled. I have a wife and five children under ten years of age and I think under the circumstances I might be allowed to once more earn my livelihood for myself and family. I earnestly trust you will aid me in securing the clemency allowed others. I remain, yours faithfully, E J West.

West's continuing struggle to clear his name reached the ears of a journalist on the *Manchester Football News*. Despite what the curmudgeonly West believed about the press, 'J R C' was not entirely unsympathetic towards Enoch – and he thought others might feel the same. On 11 October 1919 'J R C' told readers:

For a long time I have known that many people consider that E J West, the ex-Manchester United player, has been hardly done by. West himself is obviously wracked by a sense of injustice. Unfortunately this has caused him to look askance at everybody connected with the Press and that is perhaps the reason why a copy of an appeal issued by him has not been forwarded to the newspapers. It is being circulated in the big workshops such as Ford's and the workers, the majority of whom are keen followers of the game are being asked to sign the memorial.

Quite responsible men in football are of the opinion that West's suspension ought to have been removed along with that of the other players. I agree with them. Far be it from me to suggest that the FA are acting vindictively in this case, but some people are inclined to believe that West is still under his heavy cloud because he had the temerity to bring an action against the football authorities. He lost it, yet, that is not to say he had no right to try and vindicate himself in a court of law.

Whether or not his unjustifiable attack [verbal or physical? – GS] on the Manchester United manager has had anything to do with the decision of the FA to exclude him from the amnesty I do not know, but I am certain that Mr Robson bears no malice and would not hesitate to sign the petition if asked to do so.

I think that the FA have not done themselves justice in withholding their clemency from West. It is not in accordance with the spirit governing actions of this kind. It is too much like crying 'Peace, peace' when there is no peace!

The positive tone of this article must have astonished Enoch, but 'J R C' followed it up with another pro-West story a week later:

There appears to be much satisfaction that a petition for the reinstatement of West is being signed in the various workshops. One of his fellow workmen, Mr F Abbott, referring to what I wrote last week, has this to say: 'I have known West for many years and have competed against him on the running track. I have always found him a true sport and I can assure you it is high time he was reinstated. He has paid the penalty, and more, for his action, and I am quite sure the sporting community will endorse that view. I know from his own words that he was to have had a good benefit and that he has suffered the loss of it. I would like to point out to all followers of the game that no man is infallible in any sphere of life.' Having said what I have had to say it only remains to be seen what effect the petition has upon the FA. Perhaps someone interested will take the trouble to let me know to what extent the petition has been signed.

Shortly before Christmas 1919 the FA Emergency Committee considered an application from L Cook of Chester for the removal of his suspension. The request was granted. Now West was the only player involved in the match-fixing scandal who was still under suspension. On 12 December 1919 the FA Consultative Committee recorded:

The attention of the Committee was called to offers made to Players to arrange the results of matches, and that the offers had been accompanied by a promise to pay £1,000 if the results were as required. The Clubs that had brought the matter to the attention of the FA, and the Players who had at once given full particulars of the offers they had received, were thanked by the Committee.

It was also stated that the Police had been communicated with, and that while the widespread offers that had been made, all emanating from one district, suggested that it was a hoax, yet the Committee took a serious view of it, and expressed their determination that everything possible would be done to stamp out this, or any other practice that threatened the purity of the game.

Knocker was clearly not without his supporters. Perhaps his persistence and the positive response his petition was receiving were making him something of a local *cause célèbre*. On 22 December 1919 the FA considered a letter on his behalf from the Gorton Cricket Club but once again decided to take no action. [My efforts to discover the link between Gorton and Enoch West have proved fruitless. The club, based in the Belle Vue area, and which reportedly went on to become East Manchester Cricket Club, no longer seems to exist and no one will admit to having access to, or knowledge of, club records.]

Now West enlisted high-powered assistance. His MP Sir Thomas Robinson, OBE, who represented the Stretford Division of Manchester, wrote to the FA asking for the removal of West's suspension. Yet again 'No action taken' was the curt response from the FA, this time recorded in the Council Minutes of the meeting of 23 April 1920, which erroneously named the MP as 'Mr F Robinson'. At that same meeting, the FA heard from Lincolnshire Football Association that 'Wilson Holt of Barnetby St Marys FC, who was reported by his own Club for betting on a Bennett League match, which they alleged he helped to lose – is suspended *sine die*'. Did this influence the latest rejection of a plea on West's behalf?

If West's guilt was as cut and dried as the FA were making out, how could Enoch earn the respect and backing of the Players' Union, a respectable Cricket Club and his local Member of Parliament? Sir Thomas was National Liberal MP for Stretford from 1918–24. He was the product of a Liberal-Conservative pact and stood under the title 'Independent Free Trade and Anti-Socialist', although he was always claimed by the Liberal Party as one of their own. He was returned to the seat in 1924 as an Independent – but with Conservative and Liberal support – remaining there until his retirement in 1931. What would such a well-connected and influential chap have to gain by championing the seemingly hopeless case of an unpopular, shamed footballer, unless he believed a clear travesty of justice had taken place? I can find no record of West ever submitting his petition to the FA in what, as he must have known, could only have been a futile gesture, inevitably doomed to rejection.

In 1927 West abandoned his wife and six children to move south to a new Ford factory in Dagenham, staying there until he retired after the Second World War. In doing so, West forfeited the sympathy of his family and caused resentment that exists to this day. He then moved back north, to Walnut Street, Salford. My enquiries to Ford failed to unearth any details of Knocker's duties and career during the twenty or so years he was with the company, but his son, Eric, has revealed that West worked in the stores and delivered spare parts.

There is evidence that as late as the nineteen-thirties the football authorities were still determined to present West as a self-confessed guilty man and were prepared to re-write history to do so. The Football League's official 50th anniversary publication, *The Story of the Football League*, published in 1938, stated, 'In the long run, after losing his case, West admitted the truth of the charge.'

I don't think so.

On Monday 25 June 1945 the FA's War Emergency Committee gathered at the Holborn Restaurant in London. The Committee was chaired by W C Cuff and included in their ranks, Alderman A E Ansell, Comdr E W Beetham; H J Husband JP; Major General R G Lewis and Air Marshall A S Morris. The secretary was a certain S F Rous, later to become Sir Stanley. The Committee considered a number of messages, appointments and reports. It was 'mentioned that this was the first Meeting of the War Emergency Committee since the cessation of hostilities on the Continent and felt sure that the members were grateful to see the end of the war in Europe.' That theme was obviously still in their collective minds when they later tackled business arising from a meeting that had taken place on 3 and 4 May. Minute 137 was introduced:

The Committee gave further consideration to the question of granting an amnesty and decided to recommend to the Council that the following resolution be adopted: That the Council of

the Football Association wishes to place on record its deep
gratitude for the successful conclusion of the war in Europe
and has pleasure in announcing that it will consider favourably
applications from players, officials and others connected with
the game, for the removal of their suspensions. Applications
relating to suspensions by County Associations should be made
to the County Associations concerned.

So it seems that, albeit only thanks to the successful conclusion of
the Second world War, West would once again be able to apply to
have his suspension removed. By this time Enoch was within a year of
his sixtieth birthday and his suspension was in its thirtieth year – a
longer ban than any player on record had ever served. He was
obviously never going to play competitive football again. Given his
lack of recent involvement in the game, he would not be able to take up
a role as coach, manager, scout or trainer. So would he bother to go
through the rigmarole of making an application for something he had
gone to court to secure and that he felt should have been handed to him
in any case? When he had done so previously, the FA had refused point
blank to pardon him and had effectively laughed in his face.

I was initially unable to confirm whether he did apply. And as a
bookmaker, I would have been happy to offer odds against him
having done so. But no, even I had under-estimated the depth of
Enoch's feelings and his continuing burning desire for an injustice
to be righted. He did, indeed, put pen to paper to demand the
removal of his three decades of blame and shame. Surely he must
have anticipated the same response as before – rejection?

On Monday 15 October 1945 the FA Council members trooped
back into their Holborn Restaurant meeting room where they
considered requests from six people. The official minutes of the
meeting record that, 'The Secretary reported that applications for the
removal of suspensions received from the following were granted:
Messrs D Milligan (Chesterfield FC); Bendle W Moore (Derby
County); A C Pudan (Leicester City FC); W A Tomkins (Leicester
City FC); B Travers (Fulham); E J West (Manchester United FC).'

And that was it – an unprecedented 29 years and 10 months'
suspension over at last. There was no fanfare, no pardon, no apology –

in fact, no comment at all to indicate that West had served half a lifetime out of the game. One wonders whether anyone at that meeting remembered the background to West's case, or understood the significance of the decision they had taken. Presumably they would have written to inform Enoch that he was now officially permitted to resume his association with the sport of football, should he wish to do so. He didn't.

As recently as 2002, in a book called *Masters of Old Trafford* (Robson Books), author Peter Keeling claimed to have interviewed Knocker in 'the early sixties', when 'he didn't seem in any doubt that he was one of several guilty players!' By then he was almost certainly sick of defending himself to sceptical interviewers only looking to use his sentence as a stick with which to beat him and when I spoke to Peter he admitted that Knocker had not confessed to being guilty of match fixing.

When another match-rigging scandal emerged in October 1960, the *Manchester Evening News* contacted West, then 74 and living in Walnut Street, Salford. West repeated his claim that he had been innocent all along, adding, 'It is unbelievable the amount of corruption and back-biting that goes on in a dressing room,' and that, 'if a player is approached and asked to fix a game he should agree and then go straight to the FA.'

If only Knocker had followed his own advice. By this stage he was presumably reflecting on the course of action he wished he had adopted at the time – but which would inevitably have resulted in the fate which so often awaits innocent and courageous whistle-blowers – being shunned by their peers. The story was accompanied by a full-face photograph of the ex-player, wearing a bow tie and still displaying a generous head of hair, albeit lighter in colour than previously.

Describing him as the 'youngest player ever to sign as a professional' the article quoted West as saying, 'My career was ruined' and maintaining steadfastly, 'There was still four months of my three-year contract to go when I was suspended so United still owed me a benefit match.' The *News* stated, 'He still maintains he had no part in fixing the Liverpool or any other game.' It is easy to imagine West bitterly spitting out his closing remark to the *News* reporter who had prompted memories of those turbulent days. Many a less strong-willed man might have preferred not to rake up the past, thereby reminding those who would have forgotten and bringing it to the attention of others who would not have known. But not Knocker. He didn't care who knew about the incident, or what they thought of him. What was West's attitude now, almost half a century on, towards Manchester United and to Old Trafford? 'I don't want to go near that place again.'

Two years later West briefly resurfaced in the public consciousness thanks to the *Soccer Star* magazine of 28 April 1962 in a feature article 'Players and Places'. Under the heading 'Too Late', a small section said:

> Still living in Manchester and now 78 (sic), famous old-time Forest and Manchester United centre forward Knocker West suffered the longest ever suspension term. Following his part in a notorious match he was given 'life' in April 1916 [not strictly accurate] and the suspension was lifted in December 1945, all but thirty years later!

There seemed to be no obvious reason why the piece should suddenly appear other than that – perhaps, a reporter had heard that West was still going strong. Three years later, it cost 7s [35p] to tell the world that Enoch West had died. The Salford City Reporter, dated 24 September 1965, carried a seven-line announcement in its Births, Marriages and Deaths column, which charged 1s [5p] per line: 'WEST – 14 September 1965, in hospital and of 85 Walnut Street, Salford 8. E J (Knocker) West aged 79. Dear friend of Amy Houghton. Arrangements – Laithwaites Funeral Service. Telephone Pen 1414.'

West died of cancer in the nearby Ladywell Hospital, now no longer in existence, and the other cancer which had blighted his life also followed him to the grave. The obituary in his local paper referred, inevitably, to the fact that, 'Mr West was suspended indefinitely for allegedly fixing a match but always maintained that he took no part in the matter.'

A hearse and two following cars comprised the turnout for Enoch's funeral, which took place, rather unusually for those times, on a Saturday morning, on 18 September. The cortege departed for Salford's Agecroft Crematorium not from West's own address but from one in Winchester Road, in another part of Salford. According to the records of Laithwaites undertakers, still serving the local population to this day, Enoch's ashes were scattered at the crematorium's garden of remembrance.

There is no record of a request for a plaque to mark Enoch's passing. I contacted the crematorium who confirmed that there is no permanent acknowledgement that the final public ceremony of Enoch's life was played out there. However, a kind lady told me that it was still not too late to do so and sent me the relevant papers. In October 1965 Enoch's worldly goods were officially bequeathed to Amy Houghton, who benefited to the tune of £344. That's not much, is it? Wouldn't you have thought that he might have cashed in on his notoriety with a Sunday newspaper – 'I was guilty of the Big Fix all along' exclusive – had he been as black a character as his detractors have claimed? He never did, though – another pointer to his innocence. Records held at the London Probate Office in Holborn record Enoch's middle name as James, settling any lingering controversy.

As I drove home from the British Newspaper Library at Colindale, where I had spent the previous few hours delving back into the archives to search out details of Knocker's demise, I was shocked to hear of the death of South African cricketer Hanse Cronje, whose reputation had also been tarnished by match-fixing allegations. He had been killed in a plane crash.

West suffered worse than any of those who had admitted involvement. He had gone to his grave widely believed to be guilty as charged.

I wanted to try to put the record straight, at least to sow seeds of doubt in the minds of those who would otherwise accept without question the highly dubious deeds attributed to him among the pages of footballing histories, and in the dusty records of the sport's governing authorities.

8

Did It Happen Like This?

So, just what was said in the Dog and Partridge on that fateful night? Sheldon must have arranged to meet West in the pub, together with a couple of his team-mates. The meeting may have been arranged to tell them that Liverpool – or, the section of it that he had 'squared' – intended to come to Old Trafford to lose and/or that a joint effort from both sides could enrich all of them with minimum risk.

Perhaps the Liverpool lads had already decided to throw the game and clean up with local bookmakers, but were aware that they would win much more by betting on – and pre-arranging – a specific score. The odds available for a simple Manchester United win would have been around 6–4 at best. But by opting for a specific final scoreline the odds could be increased to up to 8–1. Sheldon and Co could ensure that they lost, assuming there were enough of them in on the scam, without the United players even being in on the plan. But, given that he had been a Manchester United player himself, not that long before, Sheldon must have believed that it would be pretty easy to involve a few of the boys from the other side.

Sheldon probably assumed that the infamously stroppy West would be a willing participant in the scam. But why, in fact, should he go along with it? What would have been in it for him? Enoch would be well aware that he had a considerable amount to lose. He was, after all, due a benefit match from which he might reasonably expect to pocket £500 at the very least – and very probably double that figure. Therefore, he must have demanded of Sheldon, 'How am I supposed to make that sort of brass from this match? To do that

I'd need to get over £100 on the correct score with the bookies – that would be bloody difficult, if not downright impossible.

'No, there's too much at stake for me here. The other lads can get their few pounds on and win themselves a couple of weeks' wages extra each – good luck to them, but it's just too risky for me. I'm not going to do it. I won't stop you. I might even tell some friends to cash in and help themselves. I could probably get my mate Lol Cook to put your bets on for you, but you can count me out of any direct involvement.'

How would Sheldon have reacted to that? He would no doubt have been happy that he could rely on Knocker to spread the word to those of his team-mates he felt were trustworthy and to advise those who were against the scheme to stay quiet. After all, the relegation-threatened United players would be relieved just to get two guaranteed points. That would go a long way towards keeping them in the First Division – albeit that there was no way of knowing when the League would resume, given the war situation at that time.

But Enoch would have been quite likely to declare that should anything go wrong, or word leak out to the authorities, he would protect his own reputation, and his future finances, by insisting that he had had nothing whatsoever to do with it – and even deny all knowledge. Sheldon may well have agreed, on the basis that it was the lesser of two evils. After all, West might have decided to scupper the scheme completely. However, privately, he would have been seething at West for complicating the issue, and vowing that if Sheldon himself was implicated he would take as many of the others with him as possible – particularly Knocker.

So, Enoch may well have walked away from that first get-together a little confused. Should he actively go along with it? Should he tell the authorities in order to protect himself but risk being 'sent to Coventry' by his mates? Should he do nothing, for fear of putting his benefit nest-egg at risk, except tip off a few pals perhaps? He had plenty to think about. They had agreed upon another meeting but at a different Manchester hostelry, to be held on the eve of the match. By that time they would know how many bets they had placed and so calculate how much they stood to win.

By now, too, players at both clubs would have sensed that there was 'something in the air'. But Enoch may now have come to his senses and decided that he wanted nothing whatsoever to do with the plot. When he broke the news to Sheldon they would have exchanged loud, angry words and even, perhaps, issued threats.

Sheldon might have said, 'We don't need you, your mates are keen. So just keep out of the way. Remember, if you make the slightest move to tell on us it'll be the worse for you. We'll say you were one of the leaders – the go-between, at least – right in the middle of it all. You won't have a chance to get out of it.' West may have been heard to shout, 'Please your ****ing selves, I'm out of here!' before stamping out of the pub.

And when the storm broke, would the others have dragged West into the maelstrom? Probably they did. He certainly wouldn't have implicated himself – and how else would his name have moved to the top of the Commission's list of suspects, when clearly they couldn't find any direct evidence to link him with the plot?

West suffered worse than any of those who had admitted involvement. He had gone to his grave widely believed to be guilty as charged.

I wanted to try to put the record straight, at least to sow seeds of doubt in the minds of those who would otherwise accept without question the highly dubious deeds attributed to him among the pages of footballing histories, and in the dusty records of the sport's governing authorities. First, though, a short diversion to look at the murky machinations of match-rigging worldwide.

9

Can You Hear Black Whistling?

So just what effect did the famous Good Friday 1915 football scandal have on the game? And how prevalent is betting-related match-fixing today? As far as Britain is concerned, my research has tended to suggest that, at least in recent years, while rumour is rife, firm evidence is harder to find. During the course of writing this book, I was invited by *Daily Star* sports editor Jim Mansell (a Liverpool fan, for his sins) to the Football Writers' Association Footballer of the Year Dinner at London's Royal Lancaster Hotel. This is one of the few evening events I am happy to attend, along with the boxing writers' equivalent and the Booker Prize dinner, which are also both prestigious and entertaining.

The previous year at this function I had managed to lay sports pundit and commentator Angus 'Statto' Loughran a substantial wager on Manchester City to win the First Division title, which they had achieved. Angus came over to thank me for the cheque for over £10,000 that he had recently received. I was a little apprehensive lest he decided to re-invest it on another coup. He didn't, however, but insisted on reading to me and the *Observer*'s Will Buckley and Kevin Mitchell, with whom I had been chatting, an excerpt from his about-to-be-published *Guide to the 2002 World Cup*, copies of which had cunningly been placed on every table at the event.

Looking somewhat like a preacher declaiming from the pulpit, the animated Angus was soon relating the relevant yarn, which concerned a World Cup match between Russia and Cameroon, played during the 1994 tournament. The word was that this game had been fixed, with the already eliminated and dispirited Russians said to be ready to permit the Cameroonians, who could still qualify, to enjoy an easy victory. There was massive, worldwide gambling interest in this game and the betting on Cameroon had collapsed from odds against to big odds on.

'It was,' quoted Angus, 'the biggest plunge in the history of world football' – Will and Kevin were checking their watches and looking around for someone whose eye they could catch and who they could sidle away to speak to – 'with much of the money coming from the Far East.' Angus had actually commentated on this match for Eurosport. 'It turned out to be the mother of all bloodbaths for punters as Oleg Salenko grabbed five goals in a 6–1 win for Russia.'

'Yes, yes, Angus, I remember all this, so what?'

'Had Cameroon won the match,' quoth Angus, now beginning to resemble the Ancient Mariner, 'there is no doubt that cries of "fix" would have been made through the bookmakers' grapevines, but as the result was such a massive one for them there was very little said about it.'

Angus fixed me with an accusing glare at very close range and concluded, dramatically, 'In general, layers tend to keep very quiet when they clean up, you only hear them scream when they lose.' Closing the book with a firm thud he beamed at me triumphantly and asked, 'What do you think of that – I'm right, aren't I?' It was a rhetorical question, so I didn't bother to point out the central flaw in his argument – that everyone involved in the betting industry had been made fully aware of this particular story. I had gone out of my way to ensure that this was the case – so how could he claim we had covered it up?

But the incident demonstrated the belief held by so many people that any time there is a hefty gamble or an unexpected result or, worse, a combination of the two, a fix has been perpetrated somewhere along the line. Just as it is difficult to prove that the Loch Ness Monster exists – but totally impossible to prove that it does not, so I have chosen the more difficult of two options by endeavouring to repudiate the claims made against Enoch West, rather than upholding them.

Just a week before World Cup 2002 got underway, a reporter from *The Sun* rang me at work to ask whether William Hill had any concerns about the possibility that some matches at the tournament might be fixed. My immediate reaction was to deny that such a thing could be possible as this is the world's greatest showpiece sporting event. The same fears had been raised back in 1998 when, immediately before the tournament started, The *Sunday Express* ran the front page headline, 'World Cup Bets Sting' with the sub-heading, 'Sinister gambling syndicates based in the Far East are trying to fix World Cup results'.

This type of scam would soon be rumbled if anyone had tried it. Surely, players would have too much to lose? There has never been a proven case of match-fixing at the competition – although, during one tournament, Colombia's Escobar was shot dead, allegedly by a gambling syndicate, after netting an own-goal against the USA. Oh, and everyone thinks Germany and Austria once deliberately engineered a draw. And, er... there was that iffy result when Argentina needed to beat Peru by a large number of goals. But not much in the way of hard evidence.

Other newspapers became concerned about the possible influence of crime syndicates in the tournament. The *London Evening Standard* carried a story headed 'FIFA gamble over Far East betting rings' to which I had actually contributed. Once again, these 'mysterious illegal betting syndicates' were referred to without any serious evidence to support the contention that 'with so much money riding on the World Cup there are serious fears that the game's biggest event could be open to the sort of manipulation which has so seriously tainted international cricket'.

The writer was concerned that 'FIFA has not set up any specific rules to limit the contact between players and officials at the World Cup, and bookmakers'. Peter Velappan, head of the Asian Football Confederation and a member of the World Cup organising committee, was quoted as saying, 'We have warned all the teams to be vigilant about this but I don't believe it is so much of a problem in the host countries.' The article went on to remind readers that:

The threat from Far East gambling syndicates was brought closer to home when three Asian conmen tried to fix the floodlights so they would go out during a Premiership match between Charlton and Liverpool at The Valley. Hong Kong born Wai Yuen Liu and Malayasians Eng Hwa Lim and Chee Kew Ong were all found guilty for their part in the racket which was foiled by police.

As the 2002 World Cup was played out I had reason to think back to my pre-tournament conversation with the *Sun* reporter. Co-host nation South Korea had had a number of goals against them disallowed, and their remarkable victories over Portugal, Italy and Spain had been assisted by controversial decisions. This had all led to banner headlines hinting strongly that match-fixing was involved. Not that the allegations in this case were related to betting. The general feeling was that the governing body, FIFA, were keen to see one, or both, of the World Cup hosts over-achieving, thus raising the profile of the game in the Far East and, perhaps, encouraging them to show loyalty to certain factions within the football corridors of power where the sport's future is fashioned and financed.

At the end of the World Cup it was reported from Thailand that 1,148 people had been arrested there for gambling on the tournament since it began. The 516 bookies and 632 punters involved faced three months in jail. Police confiscated more than three million *baht* (not as impressive as it sounds – that is equivalent to £47,000). But this offence has to be put into perspective. The bookies and punters had only committed an offence because Thai authorities do not permit gambling on football. By the same token, under a similar system, William Hill, Ladbrokes and Coral would be described as 'illegal bookies' yet would nonetheless be operating above-board, respectably run and fair operations.

In July 2002 I announced, on behalf of William Hill, an innovation in gambling in the UK. My company was to accept single bets on individual league fixtures. This would apply in all the countries – and there are about twenty of them – where we had previously imposed restrictions, requested by the football authorities, that this should be limited to televised matches. This was to lessen the temptation for match fixing. With the arrival of the Internet and the activities of some of the smaller betting shop operations, this restriction had become widely disregarded, thus leaving the big boys – such as William Hill – looking out of step. As the authorities were showing little or no inclination to confront – let alone punish – the companies that were accepting such single bets, we had decided that, in order to avoid being commercially disadvantaged, there was a strong case for saying 'if you can't beat it – join them'. So we did, in time for the start of the 2002–3 season.

It was not without some misgivings, however. One senior figure in the company confided to me his fear that such a move may ultimately see a resurgence of 'dodgy' matches, especially in the lower divisions where players' wages were on the decline. He reminded me of the match played several seasons ago in a League regarded as being beyond reproach. We had spotted an unfamiliar, worrying pattern of bets even before the game had started. We duly alerted the authorities, and watched as the game was played – with the anticipated result (complete with convenient goalkeeping 'mistake'). We then waited for the appropriate action to be taken… and waited…and waited…

One might have thought that the Manchester United–Liverpool betting scam of April 1915 would have caused such an uproar that it would have been a very long time before a similar scandal would taint the sport again. Think again. I have discovered an item contained in the minutes of the FA Emergency Committee proceedings held from 31 August to 31 December 1917, headed, 'Crystal Palace v Clapton Orient – Played 1 December 1917.'

The item announced, 'It was alleged that Robert Spottiswood, a player of the Crystal Palace Club was a party to the attempted squaring of the match. Upon his own admission of guilt, Spottiswood is permanently suspended from taking any part in football or football management and prohibited from entering any football ground.'

Near the end of the 1919–20 season Bury, who were in the Second Division, were sitting in fifth place with two matches still to play. Both games were against Coventry City; at home on 28 April and at Highfield Road on 1 May. Coventry were bottom of the table, behind Lincoln, but with a game in hand. Bury drew the home game 2–2 and were a goal up at half time in the return fixture three days later only for Coventry to hit back with two second-half goals from Alec Mercer, ensuring their survival and condemning Lincoln to relegation. Rumours began to circulate but nothing concrete was known for some three years until, in March 1923, the FA, which had received 'information' relating to the match, set up a Commission to investigate the matter. The FA reported on 29 March that, 'The Commission is satisfied that an agreement was made between Bury and Coventry City, allowing the latter to win.'

Ten officials and players were suspended from football for life and both clubs were fined £100. Bury's chairman and manager and four players were banned, along with Coventry's chairman, manager, and a player, George Chaplin. Years later, Chaplin reportedly confessed all, according to a 1986 book, *Singers to Sky Blues*. He is quoted as saying:

With a couple of matches left, things looked so bad that I had a talk with the chairman David Cooke. We decided that something must be done. The outcome of it all was that I went to Bury with £200 in my pocket and when I left I had a feeling City's prospects of gaining three points from the two games with Bury were not such a remote possibility.

In November 1922 *The Times* was demanding the 'suppression of the football bookmakers who prey on the gullible public'. In the same year, Crystal Palace were ordered to remove a hoarding from their ground that was advertising football betting. During the 1935–6 season, the Football League made a farcical effort to scupper football betting by introducing a system whereby fixtures would be arranged on a week-by-week basis, with clubs sworn to secrecy so that pools promoters would be prevented from preparing coupons in time for distribution. This ill-fated, badly thought out idea lasted just a couple of weeks; fixtures were leaked to the press, and attendances dropped as spectators became thoroughly bewildered by the whole affair. In 1936 a private member's bill to make pools betting illegal was crushed by 287 votes to 24. On 31 March of that year the FA Management Committee addressed the subject of 'football pool betting' warning:

The evil influence of pool betting on the actual results of matches is probably less obvious, but more insidious, than that of other forms of betting... during the last fifty years, the FA has been successful in keeping the game and the players free from the consequences of large-scale betting, and only a few cases of 'squaring' matches have been recorded: it is anxious that pool betting shall not now spread among its players, officials and clubs.

In 1949, Sir Stanley Rous – then secretary of the FA – claimed in a statement to the Royal Commission on Lotteries, Betting and Gaming, that he had evidence of only one case of a player receiving money from a bookmaker to share among the teams if a certain match was fixed. Details were, to say the least, sketchy. Whether Sir Stanley believed that the 'fix' had actually taken place is not clear, but the president of the Scottish FA, J A Lamb, told the Commission that 'many years ago' two players were permanently suspended after being found guilty of accepting a bribe – presumably this was for betting purposes and presumably in Scotland.

It is probable that Lamb was referring to an incident in 1924 as a result of which former Scottish international John Browning and Archibald Kyle, once a Rangers player, were both sentenced to sixty days hard labour for attempting to influence the result of a second division game between Bo'ness and Lochgelly. The pair were accused of handing over an inducement of £30 to Bo'ness players, Peter Brown and Thomas Anderson. The two players reported the approach to their manager and police were called in. It was alleged that Browning and Kyle were acting on behalf of an unnamed bookmaker who had sent £200 to Browning, which seems a huge amount of money to rig such an obscure game.

Stenhousemuir goalkeeper Joe Shortt claimed in November 1925 that he had been offered £50 by a bookie to throw a match against lowly Broxburn, who were duly beaten 6–2. Afterwards a bookmaker was sentenced to three months' imprisonment for his part in the affair. In 1936 there were reports that a Sheffield-based bookmaker stood to lose £75,000 if Sheffield United beat Fulham in the FA Cup semifinal and that 'fixers' might be out to target United players. Yet United duly won the match 2–1.

Striker Ken Chisholm turned out for several sides between 1947 and 1957, during which time he scored 132 league goals. He was playing for Leicester in 1949 when, he would later allege, he was told that his side's game in May against Cardiff, in the Second Division, was rigged. Leicester needed a point to avoid relegation, Cardiff needed a point to finish fourth, which would gain the players some bonus money. Chisholm claimed in his autobiography, *There's Another Way To Live*, that he took advantage of his inside information by staking £250 with a Glasgow bookmaker on the game to end in a draw at odds of 5–2. Despite the fact that the result had been rigged to end 0–0, the final scoreline was actually 1–1 – apparently a Cardiff player had scored an own goal by mistake and Leicester had had to be assisted to an equaliser to ensure the draw. No inquiry was ever instigated by the FA or Football League nor, apparently, did Nottingham Forest, relegated as a result of Leicester gaining that extra point, make an official complaint.

Allegations were splashed across the *Daily Mail* over a ten-day period from 10 October 1960 onwards when the newspaper's front page headline was 'Big New Bribe Shocks'. The *Daily Mail* 'Investigation Team' reported, 'Small groups of soccer players and gamblers have been scheming to fix the results of matches on which they have laid heavy bets. In one weekend last season attempts were made to fix four games and bets totalling several thousand pounds were laid on the results.' The article pinpointed two games which were allegedly the subject of outside interference. Swansea Town wing half Roy Saunders was claimed to have offered 27-year-old Bolton skipper John Higgins £200 to 'see that Bolton lost' its game with Manchester City. Higgins refused and Bolton won 3–1. Two Scottish internationals, Bobby Collins and Alex Parker, who played for Everton, were allegedly offered cash to lose to Chelsea – but in fact their side won 6–1.

The *Daily Mail* declared that they had launched their investigation three weeks earlier after the Football League had expressed concern about some information which had reached official channels regarding allegations of match fixing. 'The team travelled thousands of miles and interviewed scores of players, former players, club officials, backers and bookmakers,' said the *Mail*.

On 11 October, the *Mail* named Chelsea's Scottish international centre half Bobby Evans as the man who had 'tried to bribe Everton star Alex Parker to lose against Chelsea last season'. Evans, who had 72 caps to his credit, reportedly told the *Mail*: 'I had read rumours about rigging games. Another Scottish player and I decided we would try it ourselves.' They apparently offered Parker £500 in a phone call, planning to 'win some cash on the fixed-odds pools by betting on this game'. Also on 11 October another *Mail* article revealed how soccer matches are fixed: 'When a footballer runs on to the field with the aim of fixing a game, his own bet is probably no more than £20 to win £30. But by throwing the game, he may win £3,000 for his fixed-odds gambler contacts who have staked £2,000.'

An unnamed commission agent, allegedly acting as the middleman to put on bets with bigger bookmakers, was quoted as saying, 'I try to spread my bets between the six leading fixed-odds bookmakers in Britain, who specialise in singles and doubles. But it's not easy. The weight of money soon puts them wise. After the first £300 has gone on they begin to smell a rat.'

Indeed! They probably would have done then, certainly did in 1915, and definitely do today, even when millions of pounds are being gambled on individual games – such as England's 2002 World Cup triumph over Argentina on which a reported £12 million was staked. Bookmakers have had, now have and always will have such a well-developed early warning system that any unusual pattern of bets will soon be spotted and commented on. Whether it is a comparatively small number of large bets, or a larger number of modest wagers, the pattern will be detected and alarm bells will begin to sound.

In 1915 bookies reacted by issuing and circulating a handbill detailing their suspicions. Today the football authorities and the media will soon be made aware should any suspicious activity be uncovered. Discussing their revelations further, the *Daily Mail* of 11 October 1960 declared. 'One disturbing feature disclosed by the inquiry is that it is exceptional to find a professional soccer player [who] does not bet on match results. It is the sinister minority who are involved in the scandal of match-rigging on a big-money scale.'

Years later, in his autobiography, former Football League secretary, Alan Hardaker offered an explanation, of sorts, to explain this phenomenon, 'They would bet against their own team. If they won their match they picked up their £4 win bonus, but if they lost, their bet meant they did not lose financially as well.'

In October 1960 it emerged that Oldham player Jimmy Ferguson had been commended by the Football League for bringing to light an attempt by players to bet on an Oldham versus Crewe match – played, coincidentally, on Good Friday. Other betting allegations had begun to appear. Stoke's Eire international keeper Jimmy O'Neill had been offered cash to ensure Stoke were beaten at home by Norwich in August 1960. O'Neill reported the approach, and the story made the press.

The Football League had also been receiving allegations of match-fixing. One correspondent pointed the finger at a West Ham player, declaring that he had taken £1,000 to lose three matches. It was a fact that the Hammers' shock 5–3 home defeat by Newcastle in February 1960 had been heavily backed, along with a similarly unlikely away win at Brentford by Grimsby on the same day.

Another date, 23 April 1960, saw a number of surprising results. Out-of-form Arsenal beat Manchester United 5–2; Derby won 1–2 at Swansea; Bolton defeated Chelsea 2–0 and Nottingham Forest triumphed over Newcastle 3–0. Five Oldham players had apparently made allegations following a game against Crewe, whose matches were being monitored by the League. The Football League consulted with the FA and invited observations from certain players, and then submitted their findings to the Director of Public Prosecutions. But they were advised by their lawyers that there was insufficient evidence to justify starting proceedings.

No official investigation by the football authorities was ever held, despite the best efforts of Football League secretary Alan Hardaker. The inevitable assumption is that it was felt to be easier to sweep the matter under the carpet rather than risk the embarrassment of providing a damning testimony to their own inefficiencies and to the iniquities of their policies regarding payments to players, the great majority of whom felt inadequately rewarded. The structure of the game was still governed by a maximum wage system, which, in

June 1958, had been raised to £20 per week during the playing season, and £17 per week in the closed season. Even with the addition of £4 win bonuses, this was hardly a king's ransom. The maximum wage was finally abolished after Jimmy Hill (now best known as a soccer pundit) threatened to lead a players' strike in January 1961.

On 12 April 1964 the *People* ran a story headlined, 'The Biggest Sports Scandal of the Century'. This named three First Division players – David 'Bronco' Layne, Peter Swan and Tony Kay – the latter two internationals, who had been involved in match fixing. All three had played for Sheffield Wednesday when the side suffered a 2–0 defeat at Ipswich on 1 December 1962. Each of them was said to have wagered £50 on their own side being beaten, Lincoln losing at home to Brentford and York being defeated at Oldham. They each made £100 profit on their bets.

The *People*'s story was the culmination of investigations that had been continuing since 1960. The key man in the whole saga turned out to be Jimmy Gauld, a Scottish player who had suffered a broken leg while playing for Mansfield Town. He had apparently set up a network of players who were paid to rig games on which he then placed bets. He claimed in 1964 that his syndicate had been netting £1,000 per week by betting on fixed-odds coupons. The Sheffield Wednesday trio, and several other lesser-known players, were duly charged, along with Gauld. On 26 January 1965, at Nottingham Assizes, they were among ten players sent to prison for conspiring to defraud bookmakers by fixing the results of matches.

Layne, Swan and Kay were each jailed for four months and banned from soccer for life. Swan and Layne subsequently had their bans lifted and played again in 1971. Kay emigrated to Spain and had no further involvement with the professional game. Gauld was sent to jail for four years and ordered to pay £5,000 costs. The other convicted players were Brian Phillips of Mansfield and Jack Fountain of York, who both received fifteen-month sentences; Dick Beattie of Peterborough, who got nine months; and Sammy Chapman, of Mansfield, Ron Howells, of Portsmouth and Ken Thompson, of Hartlepool, who all received six-month sentences.

For the next thirty years, Britain seemed to have cleansed itself of match-fixing allegations but that was far from the case overseas. In March 1997, the *European* newspaper disclosed that UEFA had set up a 'top secret, anti-corruption committee' charged with keeping tabs on allegations of match-rigging, bribery and corruption. Secretary of the committee, Rene Eberle, was quoted as saying, 'We are actively pursuing a number of cases. In a lot of cases we run into a dead end and sometimes we get furious.'

In 1995 allegations had emerged – via the *Racing Post* – from former Marseille and Milan striker Jean-Pierre Papin that the result of the 1993 European Cup Final (in which Marseille had beaten Milan) 'might have been rooted in a betting coup in this country (i.e. the UK)'. However, the *Post* was unable to substantiate the story with British bookies.

Spread betting – in which the more the punter gets right the more he wins, and the more he gets wrong the more he loses – had been introduced to the UK. *Guardian* journalist Julian Turner was concerned that this innovation might give cause for concern. Writing in his 1995 book, *Gambling*, Turner observed:

On a smaller scale, spread betting may offer more innocent opportunities for stealing a march on the bookies. It has been suggested, for instance, that certain professional footballers with a gambling bent have taken a particular interest in some of the less central indexes: a player who has bought a spread on the number of times a trainer visits the pitch or sold one on the time of the first booking, has both the incentive and ability to influence the action without risking disaster.

Some companies were ill-advised or naïve enough to offer spreads on the time of the first throw-in. On one occasion there was very persuasive evidence that players in a top division match had deliberately kicked the ball straight into touch from the kick-off in order to profit from such a market. The bookies soon appreciated the potential down-side of such easily manipulated wagers, from both the financial and public relations points of view, and removed these bets from their list of markets.

In the last couple of seasons, football matches have begun to be 'traded' in a new phenomenon, betting exchanges, on which individuals bet directly with each other while the operator of the site levies a commission on each transaction.

In horse racing, the exchanges have prompted concerns that those 'in the know' that runners will under-perform have been profiting unfairly as a result. As yet, football betting on the exchanges has not attracted similar criticism, but it can only be a matter of time.

Three big-name footballers and a Malaysian businessman stood trial twice during 1997 over allegations that large sums of money had changed hands in order to influence the outcome of important English matches. In the first trial, the prosecution claimed that goalkeepers Bruce Grobbelaar, of Liverpool, Southampton and Zimbabwe, and Dutch-born Hans Segers, of Wimbledon, had taken cash to throw matches. Striker John Fashanu, of Wimbledon and Aston Villa, was alleged to be the go-between. Businessman Heng Suan Lim was the link between the players and a Far East-based betting syndicate that allegedly master-minded the scam. The case against the four was based on evidence of huge cash transactions said to have been made by Indonesians.

Grobbelaar was accused of taking a £40,000 bribe to throw a game in November 1993 when his side at the time, Liverpool, lost 3–0 to Newcastle. It was also alleged that he could have collected £125,000 for throwing a game in January 1994 against Manchester United – a bizarre echo of the Enoch West case – but the match ended 3–3. Hans Segers was accused of taking large sums to throw matches involving Wimbledon. The deals were allegedly set up by Fashanu, who was Segers' friend at the time. Fashanu was accused of handing £40,000 to Grobbelaar following the Liverpool–Newcastle game, and receiving £20,000 from Indonesian sources.

During the first case, in 1997, 25 Liverpool, Southampton and Wimbledon matches, played between November 1993 and November 1994, were the subject of match-fixing allegations. However, after 34 days of evidence, the case ended sensationally on 4 March when the jury was discharged after telling the judge, Mr Justice Tuckey, that they could not reach a verdict, even when permitted to come to a majority decision. The re-trial was scheduled for June 1997 and produced a climax that was even more dramatic than the original. Held at Winchester Crown Court, it began on 4 June 1997 and finally ended on 8 August 1997. The result – after the two trials had lasted seventeen weeks and cost more than £12 million – was that Grobbelaar, Fashanu and Segers were found not guilty of conspiring with Heng Suan Lim to receive and give corrupt payments from a Far East betting syndicate. Grobbelaar was also cleared of a charge of corruption, despite being filmed accepting £20,000, allegedly to influence the outcome of a match. The jury could not agree a verdict even after lengthy considerations, and so Mr Justice McCullough formally entered a verdict of not guilty. Controversially, the judge refused a plea for costs from Fashanu and Segers, saying that 'Mr Fashanu brought suspicion on himself' and accusing Segers of telling 'lie upon lie' when offered the chance to explain the £104,000 paid into a Swiss bank account. Fashanu's name would again be linked with accusations of match rigging in a series of *News of the World* articles in July and August 2003.

On 18 September 1997, shortly after their acquittals, Grobbelaar and Segers were under investigation again, charged by the FA with breaking their rules on betting. The FA commission heard that Grobbelaar had received £8,000 and Segers £45,000 for forecasting the outcome of matches. Both men denied betting on the outcome of matches and claimed they were unaware that their predictions transgressed FA Rules. Each claimed they were forecasting the outcome of games they were not involved in. In December 1997 the pair were found guilty of misconduct and handed a six-month ban and a £10,000 fine, both suspended for two years. They were each ordered to pay £4,000 costs. The media were not impressed. The *Daily Mirror* commented, 'The FA failed miserably to stamp out the betting scandal in soccer.' The *Guardian* claimed, 'FA takes soft line on two guilty keepers' and added, 'Grobbelaar walked away... with little more than a slapped wrist.'

The FA immediately ordered a review of its rules on betting and forecasting relating to those employed within the game. David Davies, at the time the FA's director of public affairs, said, 'It is essential that nobody is in any doubt that players have only one motive in every game and that is for their team to win.'

The FA had invited evidence of match-fixing when allegations were first made against the defendants in the Winchester trial, but said none had been forthcoming. Davies reiterated the request, asking for 'any evidence of wrong-doing to be brought to our attention immediately'. The FA investigation was set up under the former Metropolitan Police Deputy Commissioner, Sir John Smith. It published its findings and recommendations in a Final Report dated 14 October 1997 entitled 'Betting on Professional Football within the Professional Game'.

The then *Racing Post* sports betting editor, Derek McGovern, was dismissive. He wrote, 'If there's one word that best sums up Sir John's 27-page report it is "naïve".' He suggested another one – 'codswallop'. Colonel Pinstripe, commentator in the *Sunday Express*, sniffed, 'His ignorance of gambling shows'. West Ham manager, Harry Redknapp, himself a keen gambler, was also scathing, 'The only thing Sir John Smith has managed to do with his report is cast a terrible slur on professional footballers the length and breadth of the country.' Which Commission report some eighty years previous had fulfilled a similar function? I wonder.

Judge for yourself how comprehensive and insightful the Smith Report was. 'I came to this task with little, if any, knowledge of betting or the betting industry,' Sir John confessed disarmingly – or alarmingly. He went on:

> There were three main questions which I needed to attempt to answer if balanced and appropriate responses were to be found to what had been revealed as an issue of concern. They were:
> 1. What is the extent of betting on football matches in the UK and elsewhere, and how is it conducted?
> 2. How much betting is there by players and others who are subject to the Rules of the FA?
> 3. What problems and dangers, if any, are created as a consequence of betting by those subject to the Rules?

Sir John then pointed out something that many were, or claimed to be, ignorant of:

For over a hundred years, the FA Rules have prohibited those involved in the game betting on any football match. The current rule is at Rule 26 (a) (iv) and says as follows: 'In addition to matters referred to in any other Rule it shall be misconduct if any Association, League, Combination, Club, Director, Official, Referee, Assistant Referee or Player (in this Rule for ease of reference called the Member) is proved to the satisfaction of the Council or a Commission thereof to have done or permitted or assisted in doing or permitting any of the following:- (iv) to bet on any Football match other than an authorised and registered Football Pools'.

It came to the attention of the FA in the late nineteenth century that people in the game were betting on the outcome of matches. Therefore, in 1892 it was decided that 'neither officials nor players shall make bets on any football match, and clubs are required to take all reasonable measures to prevent gambling by spectators'.

This signalled the start of a persistent effort by the FA over the course of the next century to try to stamp out gambling. Sir John turned his attention next to the amount of football gambling going on:

Estimates of football betting revenue vary from £200 million to £500 million a year, with growth of between 3 and 5 per cent above RPI annually. Most bets are placed in shops, by mail, or by telephone. Comparatively minimal amounts (on average £2,000 per match) are placed in football stadium betting booths, a recent phenomenon. The most common forms of bet placed on football matches are based on the prediction of the match result, half and full time scores, time of first goal, and identity of its scorer. In addition there is 'spread betting', a highly specialised form of betting involving relatively few people and few companies. The betting industry, in order to protect itself from corruption, has devised sophisticated and well-proved warning and other systems that will detect and bring to notice the wagering of large sums of money or the placing of large numbers of bets on a highly unlikely outcome, which could suggest 'insider dealing' or 'fixing'.

Let me now consider the extent of betting by those who are subject to the FA's Rules. During his second trial at Winchester Crown Court, Bruce Grobbelaar, in answer to questions, said this: 'I could not tell you (exactly how players bet). I can only say that some of them used to go down to the bookmakers, some of them did it on the date of the game, and some of them give it to their friends to do for them.' Mr Grobbelaar went on to acknowledge that betting by players was common and that its unofficial nature questioned the integrity of the football match in question.

Obviously the amount of betting by players, club officials and others is impossible to determine with any degree of precision. I have heard nothing, however, which leads me to conclude that it is anything other than a widespread practice. One further possible reason why the prohibition on betting is disregarded is the feeling that such betting will either not be discovered or, if discovered, the FA will take no action.

Sir John continued:

Much thought has been given to the problems which betting by those involved in the game can create. I have received no information or even rumour that betting is used as a vehicle for corrupt practice...I am not persuaded that particular bets, such as 'first player to score' could not provide temptation to some people. Using knowledge which is not generally available to the public at large, such as the identity of a new penalty kick taker, in their own interest and therefore, against the interests of others would clearly be quite wrong. It would be a practice as unfair as trading in shares having insider knowledge or entering a competition as an employee of the newspaper running it. It should be obvious from what I have said that one of my main recommendations is that the present rule should be retained and reinforced.

Sir John pointed out an apparent anomaly regarding the present rules of the game:

I mentioned earlier the football stadium betting booth. It does seem somewhat strange that, given the existence of the anti-betting rule, such establishments should exist and that football clubs and authorities should profit from them. I am loath, however, to suggest that those attending football matches as spectators should be deprived of an activity which is harmless, or that betting on football away from the stadia should be stopped. Neither do I feel that the proximity of a booth at a stadium to players and others in the game is necessarily a temptation to them.

Sir John now turned his attentions to 'the harmful nature of betting on football by members of the FA'. He said, 'There is an obvious harm in players or officials betting on their team to lose. If a player or official bets on his team, or a match or competition in which he is playing, there may be a temptation for that player or official to attempt to increase his chances of success in the bet. This may ultimately, in the worst situation, lead to match-fixing.' In the opinion of many in the game, Sir John's recommendations were, at best, facile and, at worst, useless. They were:

1. The rule will be made more detailed to illustrate more clearly behaviour which is permitted by those involved in the game and behaviour which is not.

2. All professional players should be provided with a set of the FA Rules. It should be the club's responsibility and in the interests of football to ensure that the player has read and understood the relevant rules.

3. Bookmakers will be encouraged to report to the FA any betting on matches by people involved in the game.

On the matter of 'forecasting', Sir John was somewhat indecisive, saying, 'Although adequate, Rule 26 is too all-embracing and should be amended to distinguish between the innocent activity of public forecasting in the media where the information is available to all and the secretive activity which it seeks to address.'

One can only trust that the FA were impressed by Sir John's work – few others were. Almost coinciding with the publication of Sir John's report, Spurs' skipper David Howells was creating waves by revealing that he personally knew of cases where, as the *Sporting Life* reported, 'Opposing sides had attempted to land a touch on the time of the first throw-in.' Howells had said, 'There used to be a bet available on the first dead ball. A team who came to Tottenham and had a bet on the first throw-in won the toss and then booted the ball out of play to win the bet.'

There were suggestions that West Ham were the team involved. Spread-betting companies subsequently ceased taking such bets. A few days later, former England and Spurs star John Scales hit the headlines by admitting that he had broken FA gambling rules to win £800 by backing himself to score first in a match between his then side Wimbledon and Sunderland in a 1994 FA Cup game. Fellow Dons' player Dean Holdsworth grabbed some publicity by confirming Scales' claims. However, former Chelsea star Alan Hudson went into print in the *Sporting Life* to give his opinion:

There is a difference between backing yourself and backing your opponents, and the problem lies with the latter. If a sportsman backs himself there is no problem because he is only showing that he believes, firstly, he will win and, secondly, that it will act as an added incentive to win such a contest. However, the inherent dangers in sportsmen and women betting are obvious in that it is the temptation to take the easy route and back the opponent!

Colonel Pinstripe then became positively apoplectic in his paper on 16 November 1997 when he revealed 'the most corruptible market I have ever seen'. This was a book introduced by Sporting Index bookies asking punters to wager on how many seconds of injury time would be played during the first half of a live match. 'If players decided to fall over in pretend agony and wait for a stretcher, then a lengthy injury time could be guaranteed,' steamed the Colonel.

Similar doubts would emerge during the 2002/3 season when, during an important Cup game, a player went down injured and received treatment despite television coverage showing that he had barely been touched. Some bookies had offered odds against the player receiving on-field treatment and had to pay out substantial amounts.

In June 1998 two American players, John Harkes and Roy Wegerle, who had both played in England, claimed that they were approached to help fix a World Cup game against El Salvador. Then, in January 1999, the *Observer* newspaper reported on suspicions that an Italian *Serie A* match, in which struggling Venezia scored a winner through Brazilian striker Moacir Bastos Tuta in the ninety-first minute, was perhaps not quite all it should have been. Indeed Tuta's team-mates had seemed unhappy with his late clincher. The newspaper reported, 'On Monday Tuta told three newspapers that the reason for the bizarre reactions of his fellow players was that he had defied an agreement between them to fix the result.' The *Observer*'s John Hooper recorded League chairman Franco Carraro's comment, 'Bari were playing well and could have won, so why would they have needed to do a deal with a weaker side?' He then observed:

> A possible answer has been floating over the affair like a noxious smell. *Serie A* governs the fate of huge sums of money gambled legally and illegally, both inside and outside Italy... The Venezia-Bari game was the only one of last Sunday's *Serie A* fixtures on which punters could not lay a legal bet. Last week Venice police were reported to have begun an investigation into illegal betting.

The Leeds United manager David O'Leary was rapped over the knuckles by the FA in April 1999, after claiming to have placed a £100 bet on Manchester United to win the Premiership. The potential level of betting interest on football was illustrated in May 1999 when bookie Victor Chandler claimed in the *Observer* to have taken a single wager of £1 million on Valencia to beat Barcelona in a Spanish League game. In April 2000, the *News of the World* reported a survey by the Professional Footballer's Association that had revealed, 'over a third of players in all four English divisions admitted they have placed bets on the outcome of matches this season.' The *Sunday*

Mirror, which also covered the story, added that 'four players have been asked to fix a game' and reported PFA chairman Gordon Taylor as saying, 'Clubs themselves actively encourage betting – they have links with bookmakers in their grounds, they encourage the supporters and get commission from it.'

Following his court acquittal, Grobbelaar had sued the *Sun* newspaper, which had broken the original story, and had won, being awarded substantial damages for libel. Grobbelaar had declared, 'These football allegations came from one man and then they put two and two together because I was having phone calls with John Fashanu and Richard Lim and those phone calls were trying to get a game of football for the national side of Gambia and to go to Malaysia to help underprivileged kids and street kids, and that's why they came to those conclusions.'

But the *Sun* challenged the jury verdict. The newspaper argued in the Court of Appeal that Grobbelaar accepted money for match-fixing. In January 2001, the judges upheld the *Sun*'s challenge. Giving his judgement, Lord Justice Simon Brown said that the jury's unanimous verdict at a High Court hearing in August 1999 'represents a miscarriage of justice which this court can and must correct. There are simply too many improbabilities piled one upon another inherent in Mr Grobbelaar's case for it to begin to be credible'.

In late October 2002 Grobbelaar took his case to the House of Lords and won – but it was a pyrrhic victory. Although four out of the five Law Lords agreed to reinstate the High Court jury's verdict that the *Sun* had libelled Grobbelaar by claiming he took 'bungs' for match fixing – his £85,000 damages award was slashed to just £1. The Law Lords ruled that although it had been proved that Grobbelaar had accepted bribes, the newspaper had failed to show that he had actually let in goals to fix matches and this was why the jury had found in the plaintiff's favour. Lord Bingham said of Grobbelaar:

Until 9 November 1994, when the newspaper published its first articles about him, the appellant's public reputation was unblemished. But he had in fact acted in a way in which no decent or honest footballer would act and in a way which

could, if not exposed and stamped on, undermine the integrity
of a game which earns the loyalty and support of millions.

Things got even worse for the balding, moustachioed ex-keeper
on 26 November 2002 when The House of Lords instructed
Grobbelaar to pay the *Sun* two-thirds of its legal costs from the
marathon action, as the *Sun* gleefully reported the next day. Under
the headline, 'He Won £1 – and Lost a Million,' the newspaper
claimed that it had 'won a final victory against Bruce Grobbelaar
yesterday when he was ordered to pay us more than £1 million in
costs'. News International company solicitor Daniel Taylor
commented, 'By awarding costs in favour of the *Sun*, the House of
Lords has sent a clear message to litigants who bring libel actions
on a false basis that they may face a huge bill at the end of the
action, as well as having their reputations destroyed.'

The libel action was the third time that Grobbelaar had declared his
innocence of match-fixing to a jury – one more than Enoch West. Days
before this Grobbelaar decision, the *News of the World* had printed a
lurid headline, 'United Games were Fixed' – reporting allegations in a
new book, *Harry's Game* by former Manchester United keeper Harry
Gregg, that 'United matches were fixed – and their legendary manager
Sir Matt Busby knew about it'.

The article, though, was long on innuendo, but very short on
detail from the 69-year-old survivor of the Munich air disaster.
'Gregg says he is refusing to name names to prevent any hurt for the
culprits' families,' was the unlikely sounding caveat. The allegations
concerning matches played during the 1963–4 season were
rubbished by, among others, top sportswriter Ian Wooldridge of the
Daily Mail. Wooldridge scoffed at, 'Gregg's sanctimonious piety
about the iniquity of throwing matches for money, none of which,
without positive evidence is valuable,' and added tellingly, 'And of
that there is none.'

In August 1999 a businessman was convicted of taking part in an
Asian betting scam that fixed English Premiership football matches
by sabotaging the floodlights. Wai Yuen Liu, aged 38, of
Kensington, London, had denied involvement in a plot to black out
a game between Charlton Athletic and Liverpool in February 1999.

A Charlton FC security guard, 49-year-old Roger Firth, and Malaysians Eng Hwa Lim, 35, and Chee Kew Ong, 49, admitted conspiracy to cause a public nuisance.

It emerged in court that Liu was a convicted fraudster with links to the Triad underworld. The syndicate was behind attempts to fix two other matches, the first at a West Ham and Crystal Palace game at Upton Park, and the second at Selhurst Park where Wimbledon were playing Arsenal. In both matches the lights failed when the scores were level. Betting syndicates in the Far East can make substantial profits if games are abandoned with the result in their favour – unlike in Britain where bets are generally voided if a match is not completed.

The scam was uncovered when the two Malaysians and Liu were caught with a 'circuit-breaker' at Charlton's ground on 10 February. They had planned to plant the electrical device in order to sabotage the floodlighting. It was to be triggered with a remote control unit when the score favoured the syndicate during a fixture against Liverpool at the Valley on 13 February.

The potential for huge profits meant they could promise to pay Charlton security guard Roger Firth £20,000 just to let them into the ground. The court heard that Ong and Lim, the latter an electronics engineer, questioned staff at Charlton's ground in December 1998 about security arrangements, saying they were involved in a new stadium in the Far East. They were referred to Firth and he met them at a Chinese restaurant. After a further meeting Firth was offered the payment. But loose talk by Firth, when he offered a second guard £5,000 to stay on the switchboard at the club while the floodlights were being tampered with, alerted police. Mr Liu and the two Malaysians were arrested outside the ground three days before the match.

The first match allegedly disrupted was at Upton Park in November 1997 when Crystal Palace were the visitors. The lights went out twenty minutes into the second half, just after West Ham had equalised. The second was a month later at Selhurst Park where Wimbledon were entertaining Arsenal. Again the lights went out shortly after half time when the scores were level. A front page story in *The Times* on 21 August 1999, suggested, 'an illegal betting syndicate that masterminded the biggest match-fixing operation in British football history planned to sabotage at least eight more games.'

The Times also quoted Detective Superintendent Andy Sellers, who had headed up what was known as 'Operation Oceanlake', as saying, 'We have not been able to identify the senior figures involved – we clearly have not scooped the whole syndicate and there are other people still out there.'

As long as football survives, so will match-fixing. Even as I was writing this chapter football in China was gripped by the 'Black Whistle' affair. In England it is often said that the ideal location to open a betting shop is between a pub and a Chinese restaurant – the bar-staff and waiters will soon become loyal customers. China had just introduced its first legal system of betting on football – a pools-based game which used as its staple diet matches from *Serie A* in Italy and the Premiership in England.

I know a reasonable amount about this because during the opening season of the system, I agreed to become an adviser/tipster on the English games for a Chinese mass circulation sporting weekly. The reason the Chinese authorities gave for choosing not to include matches from their own Chinese Professional Soccer League was that they preferred games which 'offer a stable and mature format'. During 2001 there had certainly been some extraordinary results in China's second division – one team scoring four goals in the last five minutes to win promotion on goal difference and another landing an 11–2 victory, again helping them go up.

As a result, five teams were heavily penalised for suspected match-fixing, a referee was arrested on charges of receiving money to fix results, and, according to Wen Liang Yan of the *Beijing Morning Post*, 'People now think all matches are fake. Whenever a decision goes against the home team, fans now sing 'black whistle'.

A website, 'internetsoccer.com' informed readers in January 2002 that revelations of match-fixing and bribery in Chinese football could lead to reform of the country's penal code in a bid to stop the problem. 'It has been reported that the practice of the country's clubs bribing referees to fix matches has become so widespread that legal reform could be necessary to stop it. The scandal has broken with the revelations of directors of two of China's football clubs admitting to bribing match referees.'

It is possible that illegal gambling had a hand in the fixing of these matches, so I decided to search around for other current examples of such chicanery to see whether the situation had deteriorated since Enoch West's day. I didn't have far to look. The *Observer* of 14 April 2002 featured an article by Kevin Mitchell headed 'Torino's careless whisper', investigating suspicions of match fixing in a 1–1 draw between Italian sides Torino and Bologna. A Torino defender was accused of telling a team-mate to allow an opponent to score – the evidence coming via a lip reader.

The *Racing Post* ran the story and in its 9 April edition under the back-page headline 'UK layers saw cash for draw amid fix claim'. Ian Coyne explained, 'Italian match-fixing reared its head again yesterday as British bookmakers reported unusual interest in the draw before Saturday's controversial *Serie A* game between Torino and Bologna.' He said that bookmakers Bet365 even 'took a decision to stop trading the game at lunch-time.' Note Coyne's significant 'again'. During my thirty years in bookmaking I have lost count of the number of times I have been informed that certain matches will have pre-ordained results. Frequently, they do.

Mitchell reported the comments of English player Jason Blunt who had recently returned from a spell in Italy's lower divisions. 'Before one game, where we were second in the league with only about three games left, my manager said, "Calm down, don't tackle anyone today, just pass it and don't cause any trouble." I asked why. He said, "Just don't worry, this game is sorted." And we won it. There were so many fixed games it was unbelievable.'

I discovered a website called 'The Unofficial Nigerian Football Supporters Club' which was discussing a World Cup qualifying fixture between Nigeria and Ghana, and announced, 'The *Guardian* newspaper in its report last Tuesday said there is match fixing allegations in Ghana and Liberia.' Then, on 'AfricaOnline.com', I read, 'It was revealed that a Nigerian State Governor gave the Ghanaian delegation a "gift" of 25,000 US dollars at a post-match reception after Nigeria defeated the Ghanaians in the decisive game to clinch its third World Cup ticket. Both Nigerian and Ghanaian soccer officials have denied the gift was meant to influence the result of the match.' The

Liberians, who missed out as a result of the Nigerian victory, were hoping that developments would unfold that might yet get see them playing in the World Cup finals – they didn't. Another site, 'soccernet', was discussing Singapore soccer. Dom Raynor wrote:

In Singapore some corrupt players have decided that it is not the winning or the taking part but the making of money by any means necessary that is the most important ethos. Unfortunately for the FA of Singapore their Premier League – the S League – has been plagued by allegations of match fixing since it was founded five years ago. The authorities initially made football gambling illegal in an attempt to combat illegal bookmakers – the alleged instigators of match fixing. With public perception still one of corruption the FAS have taken the unprecedented step of introducing lie detector tests for players. Two foreign players charged with match-fixing await trial in Singapore and if the polygraph proves reliable other countries could follow suit as they attempt to combat the global problem of match fixing.

A 27-year-old German goalkeeper, Lutz Pfannenstiel, who played for Geylang in Singapore, where he was famed for his trademark waist-long pony-tail, was jailed for five months for accepting 18,000 Singapore dollars (9,900 US dollars) to rig three S-league matches. The prosecution reportedly said Pfannenstiel accepted an offer by another man to raise three sums of between S$5,000 and S$7,000 to bet on the matches on the keeper's behalf. Prosecutors had alleged that, in one case, Lutz asked the man to bet S$5,000 for him and another S$5,000 for his flat-mate that the match would end in a draw. The score was 2–2. His flat-mate, a 26-year-old Australian, who played for Sembawang Rangers, was jailed for five months on three similar charges.

Incredibly, Pfannenstiel turned up in England on 8 September 2001, playing in front of 644 spectators in a Unibond Premier League game at Altrincham, where he was between the sticks for Bradford Park Avenue. The programme openly revealed that he was 'recently released from a Singapore jail for alleged match-fixing'.

Legalised football gambling raked in S$200 million in bets when it was introduced into Singapore in 1999, but revenues dropped by an estimated 25–30 per cent as punters grew disillusioned by scandals, such as an incident in which a Croatian belonging to a local team was attacked by a bookie with a hockey stick the day before a match. Over on 'Internetsoccer.com' I saw the headline 'Atalanta, Pistoiese players cleared of match-fixing' – giving details of an unproven case but reporting that 'SNAI, which organises betting on Italian football, said it registered suspiciously heavy betting on the game including a lot of wagers for a 1–0 scoreline at half time and a full time score of 1–1. The match had ended 1–1 after Atalanta scored at the end of the first half to go into the interval a goal up, before Pistoiese equalised three minutes from time in the second half.'

'Guardian Unlimited' were explaining, 'Why Greece's finest striker refuses to play for his country'. Reportedly, striker Demis Nikolaidis was boycotting his national side in protest 'at the corruption' in domestic football there. Stepping down as Panathanaikos president after 21 years, shipping tycoon George Vardinoyiannis suggested '90 per cent of the population know the championship is not fair' and when the country's sports minister was asked why betting was not permitted on domestic matches he described results as 'not trustworthy'.

Off to 'football.ilibanis.com', only to find that 'Seven drop as Government step in to end match-fixing scandal'. This time I read that, 'Exactly two months after the famous announcements made by the [Lebanese] football federation regarding the match-fixing scandal, the FA has decided to drop seven clubs found guilty in this saga.' 'SoccerAge.com' was also getting in on the act with the headline, 'Indian Football Association reports Fact or Fiction?' The web site claimed:

The Indian Football Association has been the subject of ridicule ever since going public with reports regarding whether or not match-fixing was happening on the soccer field. Most of the people in the country however view the documents sub-mitted by the IFA as rigged, which prompted former stars to

say that match-fixing in soccer fields in Calcutta and in the rest
of the nation will continue unabated.

Even on the official 'Euro 2000' website it was difficult to avoid
match-fixing allegations. A history of Romanian football declared,
'They made little progress at Euro 96 or France 98. Meanwhile, with
the cream of their talent playing abroad, Romanian domestic
football is beset by suspicions of match-fixing.'

This is becoming a little depressing. Is there nowhere free of the
spectre of match-rigging? Germany, perhaps? On a site about
Professional Sports in Berlin I read the line 'after a chequered
history which includes bribery and match-fixing' referring to
Berlin's largest football club, Hertha BSC. 'Match-fixing casts pall
over V-League,' was the hot news on the 'Vietnam News' site.

Russia perhaps? Over on 'www.sptimesrussia.com' I discovered
a banner headline, 'Zenit, Spartak Accused of Match-Fixing'. The
story, written by Christopher Hamilton for the *St Petersburg Times*,
implies that the final game of the 1996 season between Moscow
Spartak and St Petersburg Zenit 'was thrown by Zenit's star goalie'.
The article asks, 'But why would anyone want Zenit to lose?' and
answers its own question by explaining, 'Zenit's loss let the club
management save money. A win would have left the Petersburgers
in seventh instead of tenth place. Team management had set the goal
of reaching eighth and set up a bonus system for achieving such a
rank. Additionally, the city administration promised $30,000 if the
team finished higher than eighth'.

No betting influence there, at least. But there was on a Hong
Kong site, 'www.icac.org.hk' which recorded that 'another footballer was jailed for fifteen months for conspiracy to win between
$160,000 and $280,000 from a bookmaker by manipulating the
results of four First Division matches in the 1995–96 season.'
What's more, there was another report suggesting that $200,000 was
won by conspirators who manipulated the result of a 1998 World
Cup preliminary match. The case involved four players who had
played for Hong Kong in World Cup qualifiers.

We shouldn't move on without recording a situation in Turkey, to
which my attention was drawn by an article in the May 2002 edition

of *World Soccer*, headed, 'Referee arrested in match-fixing probe'. This announced, 'Top division referee Sadik Ilhan has been arrested and charged for his alleged role in the match-fixing scandal that has rocked Turkey. The official is said to have been plied with prostitutes in return for skewing results'. Later in the story I note that the 'chief fixer' is alleged 'to have fixed the results and bet on the outcome of the matches abroad'. 'Refs arrested over match-fixing,' was the headline on a story on 'news.com.au' in which I read:

Israeli officials have postponed a decision until tomorrow on the possible suspension of all matches in the country following the arrests of referees on suspicion of match-fixing. Police have carried out an undercover investigation following a radio report which alleged senior officials had been involved in the fixing of results of matches for illegal betting rings.

The litany of shame seems to encompass the whole footballing scene:

Goa... 'Where have the crowds vanished?' asked Johnny Coutinho on 'www.indianfootball.com'. 'Were matches in the league fixed?'

Cyprus... 'An assistant referee accused of fixing football games has handed in his resignation because of personal problems caused by the allegations,' reported 'www.cyprus-mail.com' in February, 2002.

Malaysia... 'When a semi-professional league emerged in football-mad Malaysia, the once strictly amateur sport quickly lost its innocence. Rumors of crooked matches circulated for months before police rounded up more than 120 players, coaches and bookies for questioning. About sixty players confessed to match-fixing. The FA of Malaysia had a huge embarrassment on its hands – a scandal-ridden season in which up to 90 per cent of the games were said to have been fixed.'

In March 1999 David McDonell reported in the *Daily Mail* on the state of the game in Malaysia. 'One player heavily involved in match-fixing died in suspicious circumstances, probably the victim of a contract killing because he wanted out. He was driving home at 5.30 a.m. when his car was forced off the road... Footballers in

Malaysia can be bought as easily as a fake Rolex.' McConnell said that, as recently as 1995, 'some 127 players, two coaches and a manager from sixteen different teams were arrested. Many were charged with taking money to fix results.'

Uganda...Fixing is endemic in the country. A story by Joachim Buwembo in the *East African* in July 2001 alleged, 'So far gone to the dogs is football in Uganda that match-fixing is the order of the day'. He wrote:

Recently the managers of the country's top two clubs, KCC and Express, admitted publicly that they routinely bribed players of rival clubs and referees to determine the outcome of matches. Before a match is played, club officials send a bribe to the referee. The figure ranges from $70 for the lower leagues to $700 for the Super Division league matches. In one case sixteen goals were scored but because the paying team needed eighteen goals to qualify, the referee just wrote eighteen in the records, and nobody objected.

Ukraine...'uefa.com' reported in late April 2002, 'After announcing their intention to clean up the game, the Football Federation of Ukraine – FFU – will investigate the first case of alleged match-fixing in the Ukrainian first division.' The case involved a game between FC Polissya Zhytomir, chasing promotion, who played FC Borysfen Boryspil and duly won in a match which FFU delegate Volodymyr Foschiy noted 'was played at a very slow tempo, with very few tackles and challenges – there were only ten fouls committed in the game by both sides. It must be noted that the hosts were very passive.'

Yugoslavia...on Wednesday 22 May 2002 it was reported that 'the President of the Yugoslav Football Association (YFA) Dragan Stojkovic has reaffirmed his commitment to rid the domestic game of corruption. A number of allegations of match-fixing dogged the end of the Yugoslav First Division season with the most recent scandal concerning Partizan Belgrade's clash with Rad Belgrade in late April.' *World Soccer* magazine asked Stojkovic, 'How do you intend to prevent match-fixing?' to which he responded, 'There will be much more control and, if necessary, there will be rigorous fines. It means that those who wish to gamble with their destiny as players, managers or officials, let them do it, no problem. But they will be given a hard time.' Convinced? No, neither am I. Yet he seemed to mean it – as the 2002–3 season began there, Stojkovic warned again that match-fixing would not be tolerated. 'If we find proof of any dirty dealing the sanctions will be severe.'

On 28 October 2002 Simon Kuper (a winner of the William Hill Sports Book of the Year Award) suggested to readers of *The Times* that a betting coup was organised by people connected with Albanian side Dinamo Tirana in their 0–4 Champions League qualifying round defeat in August 2002, against Brondby. The fix apparently faltered when Tirana failed to concede another goal as they were allegedly looking for the 0–5 defeat on which the bets had been placed. 'At 100–1 a bet of £1,000 would have won the Albanians a six-figure payout. But Brondby just would not score that last goal,' claimed Kuper. The writer also cast aspersions on an Intertoto Cup game in June 2002 between Macedonian side Cementarnica 55 and Icelandic team HH Hafnarfjordur. 'I cite these two cases because it is rare to have such firm evidence,' declared Kuper, adding, 'Bribery is a matter of economics. The poor are easier to bribe.'

Ironically, Kuper closed his article by explaining, 'Many Balkan fans of Manchester United believe, albeit ludicrously, that the club threw their home match against Middlesbrough in March and made enough money from it to buy Rio Ferdinand for £30 million. If you tell them this is nonsense they look at you sorrowfully.'

Could this plethora of problems ultimately lead to the downfall of the global game? Chris Horrie, writing for the *Observer*, believes that 'people are getting fed up with football' and knows where the blame lies. 'One cause of the damage is alleged match-fixing by players and match officials, sometimes in the pay of illegal bookmakers. There is scarcely a professional league in the world where cases of match-fixing – or attempted match-fixing – have not come to light, including the English Premiership. At the same time, the advent of spread-betting – which opens up the possibility of 'fixing' a relatively trivial aspect of televised games, such as the time of the first throw-in – has multiplied the possibilities for betting scams.

'The beauty of football match-fixing – particularly for spread-bet coups – is that it is basically undetectable, and far easier to arrange than horse-doping. Given the dangers, the arrangements made by the English football authorities – and within some individual clubs – to guard against match-fixing are virtually non-existent.'

Plus ça change ... ?

Can you hear a whirring noise? I think it is Enoch J West spinning in his grave as he is indirectly accused of causing the downfall of probably the richest, most glamorous and popular sport in the world. Former England international turned pundit, Rodney Marsh, believes that football will never rid itself of the spectre of rigging. Writing on his own 'rodmarsh.com' site, in June 2002, he declared, 'You can never be certain that match-fixing won't happen again because sport is about human beings'. He revealed an experience of his own, 'Match fixing is nothing new. In 1973 a guy came up to me in a bar in Manchester. We got chatting and I assumed he was just a football fan. But then he offered me money, and money for some of my team-mates, to throw a Manchester City match. I told him to **** off! Anyone who has been proved guilty of fixing matches should be banned for life, without question.' Can't argue with that, Rod, but the vital element in that statement is 'proved guilty'. Enoch West never was – and, in my opinion, never will be.

Finally, the ultimate deterrent to potential match-fixers must be that introduced in Uganda, where, under the chilling headline, 'Firing squad – players who fix matches to be shot', it was announced in February 2002 from Kampala via the 'africast.com' website that 'after acquiring military training, players turning out for the army team will face the firing squad when found guilty of match-fixing'. This rather drastic treatment, which, fortunately, had never occurred to the FA back in 1915, was justified by an army spokesman on the grounds that this is the punishment they would face if found guilty of passing information to the enemy. 'That person has no difference with a player who fixes a match'.

10

Posthumous Pardon?

Almost thirty years after Enoch West's death, some doubts – albeit muted ones – were being expressed about his guilt, and questions asked about the fairness of the punishment he received, even if he were truly guilty. *The United Alphabet*, by Garth Dykes, published in 1994, features detailed assessments of hundreds of Manchester United stars through the ages. Dykes described West's sentence as 'draconian in its extremity'. As this is an 'official United publication' presumably the club does not wholly disagree with that phrase. Another United-endorsed book, Geoffrey Green's 1978 *There's Only One United*, featuring on its cover the phrase 'The Official Centenary History of Manchester United 1878–1978', did not delve too deeply into the affair, but on page 238 the author commented of West, 'Sadly, his outstanding career was ended by an alleged complicity in a bribery scandal on the outbreak of hostilities. He never played football again.'

Now, why that 'alleged' I wonder? Perhaps Green found it difficult to believe any United player would be capable of such skulduggery, or perhaps he had discovered some evidence that may have challenged the original verdict. On page 239 of the book, Green declared that West 'was later suspended by the FA for the alleged "fixing" of a match'. Green revealed in the preface to his book that 'the surviving minute books dating back to 1903 were put at my entire disposal and each interesting fact was clutched like a hot water bottle on a cold winter's night'. Nearly a quarter of a century on, I made contact with Mark Wylie, curator of the

Manchester United Museum and Tour Centre. He told me, 'Unfortunately no correspondence has survived from this period and our minute books tend to conceal more than they reveal.' He did, however, enclose the Minutes from a Board of Directors' meeting of 30 October 1916:

> It was reported that E J West had made a claim for 41 weeks wages at £5 per week, being from the date when players agreements were suspended by the Football Association, to 30 April 1916, also for damages and £500 in lieu of benefit match. Resolved that the matter be left in the hands of Mr C E Sutcliffe, Solicitor.

That would be the C E Sutcliffe, solicitor, who was on the Commission that had found West guilty in the first place, then. Some hopes of a sympathetic hearing from him. The minutes of a similar meeting held on 17 July 1917 recorded, 'Secretary reported that E J West had lost his case against the Football Association and Messrs Hulton & Co'. It would not seem that United settled either of the claims, for wages or benefit, but this does confirm Enoch's persistent endeavour to recover what he believed to be rightfully his.

Another club publication, the *Official Manchester United Illustrated Encyclopaedia*, which came out in 1998, again featured that word 'alleged' when briefly profiling West. Then, in 2001, along came a magnificent volume – also available expensively leather-bound for the fan who has everything – an updated variation on a theme, this time entitled *The Official Manchester United Illustrated History* – 'Celebrating 100 Years of the Finest Football, complete with a foreword by Sir Alex Ferguson.'

One of the contributors was Mark Wylie, mentioned earlier, who wrote the opening two chapters of the book, including one in which West was 'hung out to dry' by the club. Wylie writes:

> News leaked out that United's players had been involved in a match-fixing scandal. A flood of bets on a 2–0 scoreline in the home match against Liverpool alerted some bookmakers to a potential fraud. Betting on a specific score was unusual and the

sheer number of bets hinted at an attempt to deceive the bookmakers. Eventually, the FA intervened as more and more evidence came to light. As a result of the inquiry, eight players were banned for life. The deception was purely about money. As a result of the escalating hostilities the players realised that organised league football was coming to an end and they saw this as a last chance to make some money before the war ruined their careers, or even cost them their lives.

No 'alleged' there, then. It has also proved difficult to discover the official Liverpool attitude to its miscreants at the time. Stephen Done from the Anfield club's Museum and Visitors' Centre told me, 'The club's attitude over the years to potential archive material has always been – "chuck it in the bin, don't keep it".' He said that when he had joined the club a few years ago he had been staggered to discover the lack of detailed records concerning club activities: they didn't even have a full set of programmes, an omission which Mr Done has now begun to rectify. 'There was almost no primary source material at the club,' he told me. So there seems to be no prospect of discovering what was said about the match fixing scandal behind closed doors at board meetings – except that we do know the suspended Liverpool players were eagerly forgiven and taken back once they had been pardoned by the FA, which suggests that the club did not harbour any long-standing antipathy towards them.

Mr Done did tell me that although there was no acknowledgement or explanation of the affair in the Museum Visitors Centre at the moment, this is purely because of the limited space currently available. He said that he would be interested in exhibiting information on the affair when expanded premises became available to him.

Other than Simon Inglis' *Soccer In The Dock*, close examination of the affair in print has been rare. Most accounts of West's career and the pre-ordained match itself simply repeat the basic facts and assume, without much discussion of the details, that the verdict must have been sound. In his 1998 book, *Red Devils*, author Richard Kurt made a not very convincing effort to excuse United's part in the skulduggery. He wrote:

While not wishing to defend match-fixing – though the players' grotesque underpayment in those days is surely a mitigating factor – it does appear that the Liverpool players' participation was dramatically more disgraceful than United's. You could argue that there was a certain 'noble cause corruption', to use the Met's favourite excuse, in United players wanting to fix a victory: sure, they made some cash, but they also got two vital points to keep United in Division One. Some fans might even argue that anything dodgy is justified for the cause of United. And it's not as though United took bribes to lay down and die like some scummy boxer. But Liverpool did take money to lose and there was no other factor but cash involved. United paid the heaviest price, for the players we lost forever were indubitably superior, and the scandal has always been deemed to reflect more badly on our history rather than Liverpool's.

The assertion that 'United paid the highest price' seems difficult to justify, bearing in mind that, as a result of that game, the club were able to avoid a costly relegation. My own knowledge of the bookmaking world and experience of similar match-rigging or race-fixing episodes in various sports had sparked a feeling that perhaps this case was not quite so clear cut as most observers believed, so I decided to delve a little deeper. I made contact with Roger West, grandson of Knocker. Roger was born on 4 August 1942. He is married to his second wife, Joanna. They live in Stockport, and have a son, Thomas James, born in 1995. For thirty years he worked as a project engineer with AstraZeneca and is currently a quality systems manager with Green Contract Services at Sandbach. He is also a parish councillor for Poynton with Worth, chairman of the Poynton branch of the Macclesfield Conservative Association and a governor at two local schools.

Roger has retained the family football infatuation – still playing five-a-side twice a week – 'It's in the blood!' He is also a Manchester United fan, perhaps surprisingly, given that club's treatment of his granddad. One might have expected him to have turned to City! He has supported the club since 1955, 'when I cycled to Old Trafford and left my bike with Aunty Ruby, Knocker's daughter, who lived on Railway Road, next to the ground.' Roger has always believed in his grandfather's innocence:

'My grandfather had many attributes. To his friends he was a popular local hero – Roy Keane and Olé Gunner Solskjaer rolled into one. He was a first-class billiards player, and a highly social animal around the local pubs and clubs. He was also a strong character, fiercely proud – to the point of being arrogant, stubborn, with great self-belief.

'In his family's eyes he was a foolish, hard man who "frittered the family money away fighting a lost cause against an establishment more interested in saving face than seeing justice done", in the words of my Dad. In the First World War era, footballers were considered working class, so, some time after the ban was imposed, he left home to get work "down South". Unfortunately, there was a sad personal consequence. He did not return to his family, leaving my grandmother and six children – Eric, Albert, Jim, Dorcas, Ruby, and Frank – the latter mentally handicapped – to survive at a time when social services had not been invented. His wife, Kathleen, known as Kate, remained in the house they had shared in Manchester and within the family it is believed that although they had split they were never officially divorced.

'My father, Albert Basil [also known as 'Knocker'], had bitter memories of being raised in harsh conditions and, like his siblings, he had to start work early, to help make ends meet. During my own childhood my father's family said little of Knocker's achievements but rather referred to his "drinking, domineering personality and stubborn stupidity". They clearly believed the family had little to thank him for, and owed him nothing. But, significantly, I never heard them accuse him of dishonesty, or lying about the match-fixing which led to his ban. Knocker clearly maintained his innocence even in the privacy of his own home. They resented his "pig-headed foolishness" in chasing justice by "throwing good money after bad" in a fruitless attempt to clear his name. This course of action became a financial disaster, in total contradiction of the motives he was accused of in the match-fixing allegations.

'Despite all this, I retain an objective view of the affair. Such pain, anguish, betrayal, and the ultimate failure should not be in vain

– I strongly believe Knocker was an innocent man who was made a sacrificial lamb, but was too proud, and too stubborn to take the easy way out and simply plead guilty.

'As far as I am aware, Knocker never admitted to anyone, including his family, that he was guilty. What he said in public he also said in private. My dad told me that Enoch was always bitter that the club didn't give him his benefit match. He refused to go to Old Trafford again. Enoch wasn't the world's best father but he was a rough and ready type. He wasn't a popular man, even with his own family and none of his sons liked him.'

Roger recalls hearing how his father – an amateur boxer – knocked Enoch down in a fight when he had returned from London 'with his floozie' – but, critical of him though they undoubtedly were, the family never accused Knocker of having resorted to match-fixing.

'Knocker reckoned he had been set up,' said Roger. 'And even though he could probably have earned a pardon by standing up and admitting his guilt – "tugging his forelock", as my Uncle Eric, who played for Grimsby, put it – and it could have all been forgiven and forgotten, he never even considered that option.'

According to Roger, Enoch's son Jim, known as 'Jimmy' (and also 'Bunt' because of his stocky build – from the chubby children's story character 'Billy Bunter'), is not in the least surprised that his father fought so hard to vindicate himself. 'He was always very persistent, Jimmy told me. There was never any messing about with him. He always stood up to the authorities. If he was living today he would be a Communist.' Roger added, 'He didn't endear himself to the management at Old Trafford. He could have given them a hard time. There was a story that he once put the manager on his back after a particular disagreement.'

Who can rule out the possibility that his taciturn and uncompromising personality made him unpopular in the dressing-room and so his team-mates decided to stitch him up when the scandal was uncovered? They may have reasoned that when they all went off to war, it would all be 'water under the bridge'.

On the other hand, perhaps Knocker was deeply involved in the plot and was, at first, stubborn and stupid enough to believe he could get away with it. But when it became obvious that his part in the scheme had been revealed, he decided to persist in his efforts to prove his innocence, funded perhaps by ill-gotten gains from 'dodgy' sources or from his involvement in other crooked games. 'After all,' he might have reasoned, 'I have nothing to lose – I'm banned for life anyway.'

It would be intriguing to know about the cliques and enmities that existed in the United dressing-room in those days, but after all these years it is virtually impossible to discover what was going on. I thought I might have located another source of reference leading directly back to Enoch and his contemporaries, when I was told that one of Sandy Turnbull's sons was alive and living in Chesterfield. In fact, it actually turned out to be Sandy's grandson (also christened Alexander, like his father, and whose middle name is Meredith – after Billy). Alexander told me that both he and his Dad (another Alexander), now deceased, had had trials with Manchester United. Alexander added that his father had suffered during the Second World War and afterwards and had 'never been quite the same man again'. This was a double dose of wartime family tragedy, bearing in mind Sandy's sad demise in the First World War. Following Sandy's death, his widow had fallen on hard times and, to make ends meet, had had to sell off most of Sandy's medals – although Alexander still owns two of his grandfather's Army Cup winner's medals.

Alexander said his father had 'never discussed' the family scandal and so he could offer little information about Sandy's involvement in the affair or even about his relationship with Enoch West. Does the fact that the family clearly preferred to forget about Sandy's scandal suggest that they were ashamed of it? If so, would they have wanted to propagate his memory by continuing to pass his name down through the generations?

I have been unable to discover any suggestion that Enoch had a criminal record. Surely, in the months of witch-hunting that followed the match-fixing scandal, as the Commission laboured to get at the facts, there was ample opportunity for someone to smear West by 'leaking' details of any unsavoury incidents from his past. Yet no such allegations appear to have surfaced, either at the time or during his subsequent court cases. I can only believe that it is safe to assume that West hid no skeletons in his closet and had no criminal convictions.

If West had been a dyed-in-the-wool villain, surely there would have been little likelihood of winning support from the Players' Union or the local MP in his battle to establish his innocence. It is not possible to conclude his guilt purely from the evidence of the much-publicised deliberations of the Commission. And – unlike his counterparts were said to have done – he declined to convict himself. His refusal to do so seems to have cost him any chance of being pardoned by the authorities, in much the same bizarre way that a man languishing behind bars for a crime he knows he did not commit, and who protests his innocence, often has to serve a longer term. But if he claims to be guilty and shows remorse he stands a good chance of securing his freedom at the earliest opportunity.

Such a case was reported in the *Guardian* in June 2002 when a man who had served 26 years in jail for murder had his conviction quashed at the court of appeal and was set free. According to the newspaper, 'Mr Johnson could have been freed years ago if he admitted guilt to a parole board, but he refused to leave jail with a conviction against his name.' Remind you of anything? Enoch may well have been made of similarly strong moral fibre.

I contacted sports psychologist John Karter to ask him how likely he thought it would be that a man could protest his innocence for fifty years even though he knew he was guilty all along. John explained, 'You could read his persistence both ways – my immediate thought would be that he might be trying to erect a smokescreen, like a husband caught cheating on his wife who will either confess immediately, or lie until he is blue in the face. Perhaps Enoch's initial reaction was to deny it all. He then found himself painted into a corner, ultimately convincing himself he was innocent, even when he knew deep down he was guilty. However, it is very difficult to draw definite conclusions without knowing more about the character of the man.

'It is amazing what people will do to proclaim their innocence, often making it all the more shocking if it is eventually proved they were guilty all along. He may have regarded it as a slur on his image as a professional footballer to be called a cheat, and that could have been more important to him than the money he spent trying to prove his innocence.'

Prolific author and United fan Richard Kurt is well placed to give an overview. His opinion is that 'neither Sandy [Turnbull] nor Enoch [West] needed much encouragement to get into scrapes, and given that both were approaching their twilight years as that last 1914–15 season unfolded, their willingness to cut corners and take risks increased'. And why wouldn't youngsters of the day have taken risks? After all, as Kurt points out, 'The spectre of the holocaust on the Western Front naturally made most young men more reckless than usual.' Yes, but Knocker wasn't exactly a young man – he was approaching thirty.

Bookies are very sophisticated today and their early-warning systems quickly click into action when they spot an unexpected pattern of bets or an unusually high volume of support for a particular outcome. There is no reason to suppose that old-time bookies were any less sensitive when it came to developing an instinct for financial self-preservation. Am I guilty of involvement in the doping of a horse just because I back the nag someone has told me is expected to win, or bet against the one expected to lose? Should Enoch have been scapegoated merely for knowing what was being planned in the dressing room? Even if he were one of the conspirators, it was unfair that he should be the only on-field United man fingered. Quite clearly he could not have controlled the actions of all ten of his team-mates on his own. Others must have been in the know and actively engaged in engineering the scoreline.

Before this investigation began, no one had looked harder at the case than Simon Inglis, who is inclined to believe in West's guilt but is still prepared to admit, 'Because of his challenge to the FA, West was probably never given a chance to apologise, though it is doubtful he would have taken it anyway. Not once during his lifetime did he ever admit any guilt. Nor can we ever entirely dismiss the possibility that despite all the evidence West may indeed have been innocent.' Quite.

Roger West has endeavoured to discover the whereabouts of Enoch West's football memorabilia. 'His medals seemed to have disappeared. I discovered that a relative/daughter in Nottingham had once had at least some of them and I believe they may have turned up a few years back in a jeweller's in Nottingham. I have my own theory about how they may have ended up there. I believe they were flogged for their gold value.'

I was a little surprised to discover that the Manchester United Museum and Tour Centre does hold several of his medals – a 1911 Division One Championship Medal; a 1912 Football League Representative Medal (he played for the League twice – against the Scottish League in 1908 and then against the Southern League); a 1913 Robey Charity Cup Medal and a 1914 Lancashire Cup winners Medal.

Perhaps they purchased them from the Nottingham jeweller's. One wonders why United would still wish to acknowledge Enoch West as one of their own, as they appeared to have gone out of their way to disown him at the time of the scandal, failed to support him in his efforts to clear his name and even managed to avoid paying him for his promised benefit game. Indeed, it seems pertinent to ask whether the club really cared whether Enoch and/or any others had indeed colluded in the events of Good Friday. After all, crowds were down, organised national football was suspended, and the club was facing an uncertain future. United benefited from points they might not have gained otherwise – and they avoided the problem of giving West a benefit match at a time when they were facing cash-flow problems. They were also able to dispense with the services of three players and so save on salaries, without attracting the criticism that might otherwise have been directed at them by the media and public.

The timing of the announcement of the verdict of the Commission is extremely interesting, too, and could be viewed as being deliberately timed to minimise the effect of the decision. Just as an infamous member of the Labour Party's machinery, Jo Moore, would be vilified for suggesting that 11 September 2001 was a good day for burying bad news stories, so some bright spark concerned for the good reputation of the FA and the Football League may well have thought that releasing such a story late in the afternoon on the day before Christmas Eve would ensure that it got far less sensationalist coverage than it might otherwise have attracted.

This, of course, would lessen any criticism of these august organisations, and of the sport itself, which may have been forthcoming. Nor is
it impossible to believe that the two clubs involved could have been
colluding with the football authorities in order to minimise any adverse
reaction that might also come their way.

In August 2002 FA executive David Davies played down the
likelihood of such media manipulation, claiming that those were
less sophisticated days. Well, what else would you expect him to
spin, sorry, say? A statement put out on 23 December would have to
compete not only with the usual war stories but also with the general
desire to concentrate on good news at this most emotional time of
the year. At worst, the news would have captured Christmas Eve
headlines but then vanished from people's minds by Boxing Day.
And that was pretty much the scenario.

Obviously, the local papers in Manchester and Liverpool gave the
story full coverage, but on the national scene the attitude was
different. For example, on 24 December the *Daily Mirror* (offering
sixteen pages for a halfpenny) was leading with a front page
headline that would startle today's reader: 'Two New VCs:
Lieutenant Who Gave His Life To Save Wounded Man From
Murderous Blacks'.

It wasn't until they reached page 15 that readers were treated to
four whole paragraphs about the 'Football Scandal' in the middle of
the page. It was a purely factual report with no editorial comment or
discussion at all. The *Sporting Life* made a little more of the
situation, under the heading, 'Big Football Sensation', but even this
favourite read of the betting man did not have room for an in-depth
investigation.

One of the enduring mysteries of the game remains the question
of whether United skipper Patrick O'Connell was in the know. If so,
why, when the score was 1–0, did he put a penalty kick so far wide
that the referee and many spectators became convinced that he had
done so deliberately? Sue O'Connell, of Leigh in Lancashire, has
been painstakingly compiling a biography of him. [O'Connell was
Sue's husband's grandfather.] She told me, 'I believe that he did it
for devilment, deliberately missing because he knew full well it
didn't matter and that there would be another goal along in a minute

in any case! He was a man who would get into scrapes but always come up smiling. I imagine he knew just what was going on in the United–Liverpool game. At best he ignored it, but at worst was involved. With the war situation he probably didn't give a toss, after all, his own serious playing career was almost over and he knew things would be difficult in the immediate future.

'I don't believe that he had a deeper relationship with Enoch West than team-mate. I have heard talk within the family that there were religious differences between some members of the side which could have led to divisions within the team. I'm fairly certain [O'Connell] knew what was happening, and even if he wasn't active in the conspiracy he didn't do anything to prevent it.' Sue told me that, like West, O'Connell had left a wife and kids – four of them – in the lurch, so he did have something in common with Knocker.

As I was completing the research for this book, it was announced that Manchester United had signed a deal with betting giants Ladbrokes, making them 'the exclusive betting partner on its site – www.manutd.com – as part of a seven figure deal'. The company would also become 'the bookmaker at the club's Old Trafford "Theatre of Dreams" ground on match days'. Had the deal been in place back in 1915, spectators and players who were in on the scam would have been able to place their bets at the kiosk in the ground provided for just that purpose – so that the club itself would have been able to cream off a percentage of the wagers struck on the dodgy games. In August 2003 *The Times* said, 'United are reportedly exploring a deal with MGM Mirage, the biggest gaming company in the world, to establish a club-themed casino.'

Do deals of this nature send out mixed messages concerning the attitude of the club and the football authorities to their relationship with the betting industry? The authorities are adamant that players should have nothing whatsoever to do with betting on the game; yet they are quite happy to align themselves with the respectable face of betting in order to increase their earnings from the industry.

On 20 July 2002 the *Racing Post* reported that betting company Betfair 'yesterday agreed a deal to sponsor Fulham in the coming season'. The *Post* added, 'The FA have confirmed that the deal is within their regulations as Betfair operate as a betting exchange and not as a bookmaker.' A somewhat fine distinction, I think, and not one that most bookmakers would agree with, arguing that betting exchanges, which allow punters to bet directly with each other, effectively permit punters to act as bookmakers.

As the 2002–3 season got underway, it was confirmed that bookmakers and the football authorities had agreed a deal to permit singles betting on all matches, thus doing away with the restrictions on such wagers, which had reportedly existed to deter potential match-riggers. How do they square these seemingly irreconcilable positions? I use the word 'square' advisedly, because it got Enoch West and seven other players into big trouble nearly ninety years ago. Even though football now trumpets its relationship with betting companies to the world at large – the organisations involved in the infamous scam of 1915 still refuse to acknowledge the way they shamefully cashed in on the admittedly misguided, but ultimately very useful, little scam devised by a number of hard-up, frightened players looking for one final pay-day before they went off to war – and possible death.

Manchester United could not even bring themselves to honour the agreement they had made with Enoch West to give him a benefit match, while the FA decided to use him as a convenient scapegoat and to make a permanent public example of him – just because he dared to question their right to accuse him of match-fixing without being able to produce any hard evidence with which to convict him in a court of law.

The FA hid behind the rules of the game that permitted them to accuse West of nefarious deeds without ever having to back up their allegations. They wanted to make an example of him, to make him suffer for his brass neck for:

- not crawling away to accept his punishment in forelock-tugging silence and
- daring to take THEM to a court of law – where, as any bookie could have told him, West was a long-odds shot to beat the establishment.

He didn't beat them in court, yet he walked away a winner. They could never break his spirit, even though they tried to pretend they had.

Perhaps the most damning evidence against Knocker was the proliferation of bets allegedly placed in and around Hucknall, where he had relatives. Enoch may have known what was going on that day. He may have told other people and suggested that they put a bet on. He may even have put a bet on for himself. But did simply knowing what was happening make him one of the conspirators? If someone suggests that I back a horse they are sure will win, for whatever reason, and I do so, does that make me a party to any act that ensured the horse would win?

Even if Enoch knew what was going on, but did nothing to prevent it happening, does that make him a guilty man? If so, is he more guilty than any of the other ten players on his side? They all must have realised what was going on by the end, even if they hadn't realised at the beginning? And finally, even if he was one of the conspirators, he clearly wasn't the ringleader, so why should his punishment have been so much greater than anyone else's?

Another potentially embarrassing Manchester United story appeared as my book was being written. 'Man United accused of soccer kit price-fixing,' was the story under Becky Barrow's by-line in the 17 May 2002's edition of the *Daily Telegraph*, which began, 'Manchester United was one of eleven companies accused yesterday of fixing the price of replica football shirts.' Then came a banner headline on page 18 of the *Daily Mirror* of 25 June 2002 exclaiming, 'Director in Gambling Debt Row Quits Man U'. The story, labelled, 'Exclusive' by Jan Disley, claimed, 'The Manchester United director facing legal action over an alleged £715,000 gambling debt has quit the club's board. Amer Al Midani, 45, will stay on as honorary vice-president of the club in which he has 500,000 shares. He is being pursued by the Rio casino in Las Vegas which says he lost a million dollars playing roulette.' How enlightened of Manchester United to permit someone associated with the club who had been accused of an alleged gambling-related offence to retain an official position there. Enoch West was not even allowed to enter the ground again.

And then there was the even more extraordinary furore which blew up around the autobiography by United skipper Roy Keane in which he suggested that he had deliberately set out to injure a fellow professional during a match. The media reported that the injured player, and his club, Manchester City, were set to sue following Keane's comments, yet United closed ranks around their skipper, with boss Sir Alex Ferguson supporting him strongly. So, United backed a key member of their team who had, in their opinion, been unjustly accused of a controversial breach of the game's rules. Compare and contrast with 1915, when United failed to back a key member of their team who was unjustly accused of a controversial breach of the game's rules. Perhaps Enoch was just a victim of the different morals and attitudes of a bygone era. Maybe he would have been more leniently treated had the affair taken place in today's world. Maybe not, though, when you consider the hard-hearted way in which David Beckham was eased out of the club to join Real Madrid when he no longer figured in their plans.

Someone who might have been expected to show some sympathy for a man who had had to fight to clear his name is the former Wimbledon, England and 'I'm a Celebrity, Get Me Out of Here' star John Fashanu. I wrote to him to ask whether he felt any kinship with Enoch. He rang me. 'I don't see any direct parallels with my own situation,' he said. Fashanu, who at the time was involved in a takeover bid for Second Division club, Northampton Town, told me he had been approached by an internet bookie to front an advertising campaign which would have him saying to the camera, 'That just could NOT be fixed'. He didn't do it because he was not in the country at the time. 'I'm glad you've brought the matter to my attention,' he said, 'it seems a very interesting case. But I don't think I'd want to become involved in any campaign on West's behalf.'

I thought this attitude a little surprising, bearing in mind comments he later made to football magazine *Four Four Two* in its October 2002 edition in which he was asked, 'What effect did being implicated in a match-fixing scandal have on your life?' Fashanu's quoted response was:

Every footballer has a period when they think they're untouchable. Your face becomes your passport and I think it was a lesson. It showed me how many people have been con-victed of crimes they haven't committed... It's strengthened me a lot and made me appreciate life, but it damaged my bank balance by £1 million in legal fees. But it wasn't about the money, it was about being able to get on with your life, knowing you've been through the mill and come out clean.

You would expect Enoch to endorse most of that. I also wrote to Bruce Grobbelaar – coincidentally, on the day that he launched his House of Lords challenge against a Court of Appeal verdict (see Chapter 11). He failed to reply.

Roger West and I agreed that we owed it to Enoch to make a genuine attempt to clear his name posthumously or, at the very least, to win him an official pardon from the FA, who had made him serve a thirty-year suspension even though they effectively forgave everyone else involved within five years. I wrote to Adam Crozier, then the FA's chief executive, who responded, 'Many thanks for your letter of 1 July with regards to Enoch West. I have passed your note on to David Davies and asked him to reply to you once he has had a chance to consider. Kind regards.' A neat piece of buck passing, handing the matter on to his side-kick.

I wrote to Manchester United, requesting that they now honour – at least financially – their guarantee to Enoch West of a benefit match, and that they also make a payment equivalent to the amount of the outstanding wages he was refused. Their reply, although pretty adamant, was couched in interesting terminology. It was signed by Manchester United's secretary, K R Merrett, who wrote on 19 July 2002:

Mr Kenyon [Club Chief Executive] has asked me to acknowledge receipt of your letter dated 26 June 2002. The reason I have taken so long in replying is that we have been investigating the events to which you refer. I have to say this query was certainly out of the ordinary and made for a much more interesting archive search than is normally the case. We believe given the circumstances that we cannot accept that we have any moral obligation to stage a benefit in respect of Enoch West.

A reply raising more questions than it answered. No surprise that the request for a benefit would be turned down, but interesting that the United obligation was referred to as a 'moral' one – was this deliberate, so as not to indicate any opinion regarding a possible legal obligation? No mention, either, of Enoch's outstanding wages. And, reading between the lines, the fact that Mr Merrett had found the search for information of interest suggested that club archives might, after all, contain information that would substantiate their decision to refute the benefit request. If so, I wondered, had he unearthed anything I had been unable to discover.

Another letter was clearly called for – only to produce a predictable, deafening silence. So, I rang Mr Merrett who was, if not evasive, somewhat cautious, indicating that any further information he might be able to supply would have to come via the club museum. I got the impression that nothing would be forthcoming and that he did not wish to get deeply involved in prising open this particular container of wriggly creatures.

I finally heard from David Davies, who admitted that he was intrigued by the case, and also indicated that he had as yet been unable to locate any hard evidence to support the FA's stance of 87 years earlier. He hadn't even been aware that Knocker had eventually had his suspension lifted. When I confirmed that fact to him he seized upon it and asked, 'Well, what else do you want us to do now?'

I explained that Roger and I wanted some acknowledgement that the FA finally accepted that West should never have been suspended for longer than anyone else accused, if indeed he should ever have been named as one of the guilty men. We felt the FA should award him a posthumous pardon and own up to the fact that they had only insisted on keeping his suspension in place for having the gall to take them on in a court of law.

Davies confirmed that there was still very much a feeling among the football powers-that-be that 'football problems should be dealt with by the football fraternity'. He asked whether I could show him more information, so I wrote him another letter, including with it a summary of the case in defence of Enoch West. I wrote saying: 'Thank you for taking the trouble to call me yesterday and for showing interest in my efforts to rehabilitate the reputation of Enoch West. I think the main thrust of my quest is that there was never sufficient evidence available for Enoch to be suspended for life in the first place, but that once he had been he should certainly have had that suspension removed at the same time as the other seven suspended with him. To have remained suspended and disgraced for thirty years was a massive, outrageous injustice – the worst I have come across in the history of British football.'

I also asked Davies for 'an acknowledgment on behalf of the FA that West is due at the very least an apology for being differently treated' and told him that 'the body of evidence and information I have assembled would render it impossible for any jury to conclude that West could be convicted beyond reasonable doubt'. With my letter sitting on Davies' desk awaiting a response, I was most interested to read in the *Daily Telegraph* of 29 August 2002 the following report by Charlie Norton and Clemmie Moodle:

Adam Crozier, the chairman of the Football Association, yesterday defended the inconsistent decision to shorten the three-year ban on Leeds defender Jonathan Woodgate in time for Monday's selection of the England squad to play Portugal in a friendly two days later. Woodgate was found guilty of causing an affray after a second trial in December 2001 and, though England fans who similarly misbehave are banned for three years, Woodgate is now available to represent England two years and nine months since his ban was initiated. 'Our decision hasn't changed,' said Crozier, 'We felt that you couldn't go on punishing people for ever'.

I'll just run that quote past you again. Discussing a decision to shorten a suspension from three years to two years nine months, Mr Crozier said, 'We felt that you couldn't go on punishing people for ever.'

I waited for three more weeks before chasing David Davies up to discover whether he was close to making some kind of decision. He was away on business in Zurich, said his secretary, but she would mention my call to him and try to get back to me later in the day. She did call back, informing me that 'Mr Davies would be in contact' with me 'very shortly'. Then, on 16 September I was a little surprised to receive a second missive from Manchester United

Secretary, Ken Merrett, although not so surprised at the sentiments expressed with regard to West's unpaid wages – 'We do not believe that Manchester United have any responsibility,' he wrote.

No responsibility to a campaign to restore to respectability one of United's foremost pre-First World War performers – the only United player ever to be convicted of match-fixing in a game in which he had taken part? A neutral observer might think that with a little foresight and PR nous the club could emerge with great credit – perhaps settling the unpaid monies with a charitable gesture of some sort, and welcoming a campaign which had demolished the charges against one of their most capable strikers, tarred for almost a century by the brush of scandal. But no. No moral obligation. No responsibility. And they wonder why people believe United suffer from a siege mentality.

To their credit, though, United did agree to let me have a photograph of the medals won by West that are now displayed at the club museum.

I suppose United feared a costly claim if they were to accept any responsibility for West's treatment back then. After all, what sort of transfer fee and wages could Enoch West have commanded today? When he signed for United, West was the regular top scorer in a Premiership-equivalent side, and had headed the overall divisional scoring chart. He was United's top scorer in 1910–11, again in 1911–12 and in 1912–13. He was third top scorer in 1913–14 and second in 1914–15. During these seasons he was on the fringe of full international honours – and remember that far fewer such matches were played then. You could bracket him with, say, Kevin Phillips or Les Ferdinand – just short of absolute world class, but a player who, at his best, would now command a high seven- or low eight-figure fee, and wages of at least £10,000 per week. On that basis, perhaps I can understand United's reluctance to accept Enoch's innocence officially. I wonder whether they believe that his grandson Roger may demand compensation for the forty weeks' wages remaining of his contract – £200 at 1915 rates, but up to half a million pounds at 2003–04 levels!

At the time that I was in correspondence with Old Trafford, David Beckham – still probably expecting to be there for years to come – was floating the idea of United playing England for his testimonial match – a game which, it was predicted, could raise £2 million, which the England skipper would donate to childrens' charities. At a conservative guess, Enoch's ungranted benefit would have a seven-figure value by today's standards. But maybe such sums would be only fair recompense for the nearly ninety years of disrepute and calumny heaped on Knocker's blameless reputation?

When all is said and done, Manchester United could probably afford such a gesture. As the *Daily Express* reported on 1 October 2002, 'Reaching the semifinals of the Champions League and a profitable year on the transfer markets boosted profits for the Red Devils 48 per cent to £32.3 million.' And they kicked Knocker out for an unproven bet worth seventy quid.

Meanwhile, Roger West was beavering away trying to uncover more family information. 'I have been on a mission to find other relatives,' he told me in August 2002. 'The news is mixed. I discovered the last known addresses of Enoch's children, Ruby and James – but when I went to visit, the current residents reported that both had moved to sheltered homes about eight years ago and were subsequently believed to have died. One neighbour sadly commented that Ruby left her estate to her only daughter, Kathleen, who had not replied to any of her letters for several years.'

The Professional Footballers' Association were sympathetic towards our quest. The chief executive, Gordon Taylor, wrote, 'I would also certainly be part of the support for you to establish the innocence of Enoch West if the evidence is strongly in favour of this.' After I supplied the PFA with additional details, Gordon Taylor strengthened his support for our campaign by writing, 'I am pleased to give you the PFA's backing to rehabilitate his reputation and the injustice which clearly seems to have been done to him. I appreciate your efforts in this regard in trying to establish a pardon for him and the clearing of his name for the benefit of his family.'

If such a case were to emerge today, there is no doubt that the police would be asked to investigate. If concrete evidence had been available in 1915, wouldn't police action have followed automatically? I contacted Merseyside Police to check whether they hold any records of such an investigation. Spokesman Tony Mossman told me they didn't. Greater Manchester Police were also unable to produce any. There are no newspaper reports of police enquiries that I can unearth. This, I would suggest, is further evidence, albeit circumstantial, in favour of Enoch West.

On 23 October 2002 I received important news. An e-mail came from David Davies announcing, 'I am arranging for all the material in this case to be presented to the Disciplinary Committee of the FA'. A brief note, but also an historic breakthrough for my campaign. After 87 years the FA were willing to consider that they might have erred, and that the original case against West may have been unsafe. As far as I am aware, giving a deceased player a posthumous hearing is an unprecedented situation. I immediately responded to David Davies, offering to appear in front of the Disciplinary Committee on Enoch's behalf, and asking for some idea of the time-scale involved.

News of the FA's unique decision was made public in the *Sun* on 9 November 2002, by their chief reporter, John Kay, a good friend of mine. We hoped it might prompt someone to dredge up from a neglected corner of their brain some long-forgotten first- or second-hand memories of Knocker. John's story headed one of the inside pages of the paper, accompanied by a small photo of Enoch West. On that same day – to Roger West's chagrin – Manchester United crashed to a surprise 1–3 defeat to Manchester City in what was to be the last League game between the two at Maine Road. The papers also carried news that United were set to sue Italian club Lazio for non-payment of the eight-figure fee due from the transfer of Japp Staam.

Then came an extraordinary development. John passed on to me an e-mail from *Sun* reader Dave Bowers telling me that he and wife Sylvia 'live opposite (Enoch's) son, Charles Eric West, who was also a pro footballer and is 93-years-old today and is still fit and active.' I couldn't quite believe that this could really be Knocker's eldest son, who was known by his second name – Eric. Further information arrived from Dave Bowers: the son's address – in Thornton-Cleveleys, Lancashire – and phone number.

I was about to talk to a person – probably the only person surviving – with direct, first-hand experience and knowledge of Enoch West. After some initial confusion, as I explained to Eric that the reason I do not have a Scottish accent is that I am not actually the former Everton and Scotland striker Graeme Sharp, my first question cut straight to the chase – 'Do you believe your father was innocent or guilty?' 'How the bloody hell should I know?' was the blunt response.

To this day, Eric clearly has mixed feelings towards the man who had walked out, leaving his wife Kate [maiden name Katherine Phyllis Reeve – and Reeve was the name Knocker used when he tried to beat his ban by playing under an assumed name] to raise the children alone. As we chatted for almost half an hour it became obvious that he affects an indifference towards the man who, he says, 'I had very little to do with', but who must have had a significant, albeit relatively short-lived, influence on him.

Eric remembers that Enoch was from a family of ten – five boys, five girls, and that his father had died relatively young. He recalls that he 'would bet on anything – horses and football in particular' and that he was also 'a big drinker'. I had just finished reading Niall Quinn's autobiography in which the Republic of Ireland striker reveals that he, too, would bet on anything and that he was a big drinker. Yet Eric has never inherited either of these traits, even though at one time he ran a pub – 'because my wife Maud wanted me to'.

Eric became known as Knocker as well, and was a promising footballer himself as a youngster. 'Arsenal wanted me – Herbert Chapman wrote to me twice, telling me he had arranged to have me watched. But Dad wouldn't let me have anything to do with them.' (Eric laughed but didn't deny it when I suggested that perhaps Enoch didn't want him to have anything to do with 'southern softies'.) 'I trained with Manchester United, but eventually signed and played at wing half for Grimsby,' – where he earned £1.50 a week – 'but I was crocked after sixteen games.' He also turned out for Barnsley and Wrexham, and grew taller than his old man – to 5ft 10½in.

When the scandal broke, Eric's father, who still walked about the area challenging anyone to condemn him to his face, told his son aggressively, 'Don't hide, you tell' em who you are.' Eric felt self-conscious and believed that people were talking about Enoch, believing 'that he let the club down, sold them out'. But Knocker was defiant, unrepentant.

'I never heard him admit any guilt. It wasn't discussed that much in the family, and when Dad walked out on us, leaving Mum to look after us on her own, we had very little more to do with him. He wasn't very popular with us. He was no longer welcome at home. Not everyone believed he was guilty, though, and I do remember him standing outside Old Trafford, handing out pamphlets from a Gladstone bag, and declaring his innocence to anyone who would listen.'

When Knocker fell ill with the cancer that would eventually kill him, Eric recalled one of his brothers paying him a visit in hospital. 'He said he barely recognised him. When my Dad died I didn't feel sad – he'd lived away from us for so long, and had no contact at all.'

Yet, Eric, who recalled being at school with the children of Enoch's team-mate Sandy Turnbull, still retains memories of seeing his Dad play, watching from the Directors' Box at Old Trafford, and of being taken out with him when he began working as a delivery man at Fords in Trafford Park. 'I remember hanging out of his van once in thick fog trying to direct him.'

Eric served in the Army during the Second World War, followed by many years working in the accounts department at a brewery, before retiring to run a pub, a newsagent's and a tobacconist/sweetshop. Eric, widowed ten years ago, has a daughter living in Torquay – 'she wants me to go down there with her, but she's not been too well' – and a geologist son, David, in Canada, who is no great football fan, although Eric recalls him once turning out as the only white member of a team in Zambia.

I asked the still alert Eric who he supported. 'A wife and two kids,' he shot back instantly. 'Would you be pleased if your father's name was cleared?' 'Wouldn't matter much to me,' he said, not entirely convincingly, but revealing the lasting hurt inflicted by Knocker – the unfeeling abandonment of his family.

The *Manchester Evening News* picked up on the story from the *Sun*, reporting that, 'A Manchester United soccer ace accused of match-fixing nearly ninety years ago could be cleared, thanks to an investigation by a betting expert.' This story yielded a phone call from a lady telling me that she was related to and knew the whereabouts of Enoch's daughter Ruby's sister-in-law. She is in a nursing home. I wrote to her to ask whether she had any memories of Ruby and/or Ruby's father. No reply, though.

Meanwhile, the stately progress towards the FA hearing continued. Disciplinary head Alan Wilkes emerged as the man responsible for its conduct. I wrote to him asking for some idea of the timetable involved as Christmas loomed on the horizon. Another little twist saw Joe Evans, from MUTV, Manchester United's dedicated television channel, calling to ask me for an interview about Enoch and the book. Joe was not well informed about Knocker's place in the pantheon of Old Trafford heroes, but his interest soared when I told him the club museum held West memorabilia and details of the player's goal-scoring exploits. I somehow forgot to tell the now enthusiastic Joe that I was hoping to claim some hefty compensation from United, should the FA clear Enoch, and he volunteered to chivvy the Disciplinary Committee along. He also mentioned that David Davies is a keen Manchester United supporter.

Lawyer Nick Brocklesby rang me on 21 November 2002. 'I am seconded to the FA, and I have just received details of the case you are pursuing. I've been told to investigate and find out whether we can re-open the case. Can you help me out with some points?'

The buck had moved on yet again, but at least Nick was confident that things could be sorted out fairly swiftly. He was particularly keen to discover whether Enoch had had the option of an appeal against the original Commission decision. A week later I again spoke to Brocklesby, who assured me that he had passed his recommendations on to 'senior executives' and he anticipated that I should receive an official response within the next few days.

On 1 December Manchester United went to Anfield to play Liverpool in a vital Premiership match. Liverpool keeper Jerzy Dudek made one of the most horrendous blunders of the season – letting an innocuous headed back-pass squirm out of his hands and through his legs. It allowed Diego Forlan to score the first goal of a tight game that the visitors went on to win 1–2.

Following the surprise departure of Adam Crozier, David Davies had assumed the position of the FA's acting chief executive and so his workload must have assumed massive proportions. But he found time to write a comprehensive analysis of the Enoch West case, which arrived on my desk less than 24 hours after Dudek's disaster:

Dear Graham, I refer to your various letters in relation to Mr West, which were sent to Mr Crozier dated 1 July, Mr Wilkes dated 11 November, and myself dated 20 August and 22 October 2002. I, along with other individuals here at The Football Association, have now considered your submissions and requests in detail. In answering these submissions, I think it is sensible to first set out a summary of the material facts relating to Mr West's suspension from football.

Summary of the Material Facts

In 1915, an independent commission was appointed by The Football Association to investigate the alleged 'squared' fixture between Manchester United and Liverpool which took place on 2 April 1915.

In December 1915 an Emergency Committee of The Football Association, in light of a review of the report of that commission, permanently suspended Mr West and others from taking any part in football or football management. It seems that Mr West did not at this time look to appeal this suspension directly to the Football Association.

In 1919 after the conclusion of the First World War, the Council of The Football Association passed a unanimous resolution that applications received from players and others, for the removal of their suspensions, would be considered favourably.

An Emergency Committee subsequently adopted this resolution, and removed the suspension of all players involved with the above mentioned fixture, other than the suspension of Mr West. In July 1917 Mr West commenced legal proceedings against The Football Association and various newspapers, seeking damages for libel and also the dismissal of his suspension. I understand that Mr West's case failed at first instance and on appeal.

In June 1945, after the conclusion of the Second World War, the Council of The Football Association passed a further unanimous resolution that applications made for the removal of players' suspensions would again be considered favourably. In October 1945, an Emergency Committee granted the application for the removal of Mr West's suspension.

Conclusion

Your letter sent to Mr Crozier dated 1 July 2002 requests a 'posthumous apology and/or pardon (he was only granted a lifting of his suspension) from the FA to a man against whom no significant evidence was ever produced in public.'

The formal proceedings of the Emergency Committee were conducted in confidentiality, as indeed are the current proceedings of the Disciplinary Commission. The very nature of the proceedings brought before the Committee demanded this. It is, however, absolutely clear that the independence and impartiality of the Committee was not in any way compromised by the fact that the evidence submitted to the Committee remains outside of the public domain.

Your assertion that the suspension of Mr West was only lifted, rather than dismissed, is indeed correct. The Football Association has not, at any stage, reviewed on appeal the original decision of the Emergency Committee.

Mr West's suspension was lifted in light of the general amnesty at the conclusion of the Second World War, as a matter of compassion, rather than on appeal. After consultation with the Disciplinary Commission, I have concluded that there no longer exists any procedural opportunity to enable Mr West's case to be heard on appeal some 87 years after the original decision at first instance.

I should also state that, while the report of the independent commission and any documented reasons for the original decision of the Emergency Committee no longer exist within our archived records, I have no reason to doubt either the veracity of the commission's investigations or the considered decision of the Emergency Committee.

Therefore, neither I, in my role as Acting Chief Executive of The Football Association, nor the Disciplinary Commission itself, can grant any posthumous apology and/or pardon to Mr West. Any such apology and/or pardon would undermine the original decision of the Emergency Committee. I am not aware of any reason or circumstance which would justify undermining that decision.

I am very much aware that this matter is one in which you have invested much time and endeavour. As a result, I too have given time and effort trying to find a positive solution. At the least, I hope you recognise the seriousness with which I have treated your request. Yours sincerely... David Davies, Acting Chief Executive.

So, there you have it. Davies cleverly disguised the fact that any evidence in the possession of the Commission was never produced at the time and almost certainly no longer exists – if it ever did. No matter, suggested DD, 'it is absolutely clear that the independence and impartiality of the Committee was not in any way compromised'. Clear, perhaps to Davies. Not to me.

He also said that although the Committee's evidence and documentation 'no longer exist within our archived records' that is no reason to doubt 'the considered decision of the Emergency Committee'. And that would be because, er... you say so, would it? Possibly the contents of this book might just change his mind – but, given that any change of opinion could result in retrospective legal action against both the FA and Manchester United, I'd say that it is somewhat unlikely.

You must judge for yourself whether I have made a plausible case in defence of Enoch's previously unblemished name, but I am confident that at the very least I have established that there is little or no genuine evidence which can be interpreted as conclusive proof of the guilt of Enoch West as charged.

11

Extra Time

What happened to those players and officials who took part in the match but were never accused of being involved in the plot?

The other members of Manchester United:

John Robson, the Manchester United manager, remained in charge during wartime, supervising games during the hostilities. He stayed as boss until 1921 when the club's fortunes began to decline. He then carried on as assistant to his successor, John Chapman, for a short period.

Bob Beale was born on 8 January 1884. He guested for Arsenal during the First World War and although he remained on United's books after the conflict he turned out only in the reserves, once travelling from his native Maidstone to Old Trafford to play in a 6–1 win against Southport Central. Beale played a total of 105 matches for Manchester United. He later turned out for Gillingham and Maidstone United. He retired from football in 1921 and died in Dymchurch, near Folkestone, on 5 October 1950, aged 66.

Joe Haywood took up rugby during the First World War, despite still being officially listed as a Manchester United player. He played ten games for United in the Lancashire Section Principal Competition during the 1918–19 season. Hayward was transfer-listed at a cut price in May 1920, having chalked up 26 League appearances for United, but seems not have found a new club.

John Hodge (or more likely his brother James, the available records are inconclusive) played eleven games for United in the Lancashire Section Principal Competition during the 1918–19 season, scoring five times. A one-club man, he notched up thirty League games for United before he was put up for transfer on 28 May 1919 for £25. He does not seem to have played in League football again.

James Montgomery was born in Craghead. He joined Manchester United in 1914, from Glossop for whom he played 67 games and scored one goal. He made 27 appearances for United and scored once – finally becoming a junior coach at Old Trafford before leaving for Crewe Alexandra in 1921.

Joe Norton was born in Leicester in 1890. He joined the army during the First World War, guesting for Nottingham Forest during the 1915–16 season and winning the Principal and Subsidiary Midland tournaments with them. Norton also joined the invincible 46th Divisional team, who never lost a game in France. He was transfer-listed by United for £100 in May 1919 and signed for Leicester City. After one season and eleven games, he moved to Bristol Rovers where he scored in their first Football League victory on 1 September 1920 – a 3–2 win over Newport County. He notched up 38 appearances and two goals for the Rovers before playing for Swindon, Kettering, Atherstone, Hinckley Utd and Ashby Town during the twenties.

Arthur Potts was born in Cannock on 26 May 1888. He served in the army during the First World War and, while billeted at Southport, turned out for local side Central during the 1915–16 season. He returned to Old Trafford after the hostilities, playing in the opening League match of the 1919–20 season, but then faded out of contention, having played for the club 27 times and scored five goals. After being transfer listed for £100 in May 1920, he joined Second Division Wolves, for whom he made 35 appearances and scored nine goals. He helped the side reach the April 1921 FA Cup Final at Stamford Bridge, where they lost 1–0 to Spurs. Potts moved on to Walsall, Bloxwich Strollers and Dudley Town, playing until 1931, by which time he was in his early forties. He died in South Staffordshire in January 1981 in his ninety-third year.

Walter Spratt was born in Huddersfield in 1892. He played twelve times for Manchester United until the First World War, when he worked in a Sheffield munitions factory. He was hospitalized through a football injury and discharged in September 1919. Returning to United, Spratt played just one more first team game for the club, a 1–0 defeat against Arsenal in February 1920, before being released at the end of the season. He then played for Brentford, Sittingbourne and amateur side Elsecar Main in Sheffield.

The other Liverpool players:

Tom Watson, the manager, died in May 1915 without ever discovering what had really gone on during the match.

John McKenna, the chairman, remained a director of the club until 1922. From 1910 until his death in March 1936, aged 81, he was president of the Football League.

William ('Willie') Banks was born in Cramlington in 1893. He added to his 26-match, six-goal pre-War tally when he turned out for Liverpool in wartime competitions. He went on to join Second Division Fulham for £600 where he played forty games and and scored a dozen goals. He finally lost his place to England international Danny Shea and vanished into football obscurity.

Philip Bratley was born in Rawmarsh on 26 December 1880. He briefly played for Doncaster Rovers and then Rotherham County before joining Barnsley, where he had played 107 games and scored seven goals. In May 1914 Bratley joined Liverpool, where he played just thirteen games. There are few records of his subsequent career, although it is known that he rejoined Rotherham County for ten games in the 1919–20 season before moving to Worksop Town. He died in 1962 in his 83rd year.

Ephraim Longworth was born in Halliwell on 2 October 1887. He stayed with Liverpool from 1910 until 1927–8, playing until he was 40, having made around 350 appearances, but without scoring. He then joined the coaching staff. He was the first Liverpool player to captain England, winning five caps. He died on 7 January 1968, aged 80.

Donald McKinlay was born in Newton Mearns on 25 July 1891. He skippered Liverpool when they won consecutive Championships – in 1922 and 23 – and was twice capped for Scotland. He was with Liverpool from 1910–29, making over four hundred appearances and scoring over thirty goals, before leaving to join Prescot Cables. He later became a licensee in Liverpool. McKinlay died on 16 September 1959, aged 68.

Jimmy Nicholl was born in Port Glasgow. He joined Liverpool from Middlesbrough, where he had played 52 games and scored thirteen goals. At Liverpool he again played 52 games, this time scoring twelve goals, before disappearing from the game during the First World War.

Fred Pagnam was born in Poulton-le-Fylde on 4 September 1891. He sparkled for Liverpool in wartime competitions, hitting 42 goals in 48 games during the 1915–16 and 1916–17 seasons. He then moved to Arsenal in 1919 for £1,500 (where he played fifty League games and scored 26 goals). He signed for Cardiff in March 1921 for a hefty £3,000, where he played 27 games and scored six goals, and later in the same year moved to Watford, where the £1,000 fee made him their first four–figure player. After playing 144 games and scoring 67 goals for Watford, he became club manager from 1926–9. He was later appointed Turkey's national coach before going on to coach in Holland. After leaving the game, he entered the licensed trade. He died on 7 March 1962, aged 70.

Elisha Scott was born in Belfast on 24 August 1894. He remained at Liverpool until 1934 having played 467 games. While he was at Liverpool, Everton offered £250 for him but a flood of protest letters from fans persuaded the club to reject the bid. He then become a successful player–manager of Belfast Celtic, where he remained until the club folded in 1949. Scott won four caps for Ireland and 27 for Northern Ireland, making the last of his international appearances in 1936, at the age of 41 (by which time he had already been diagnosed with a heart problem). He died on 16 May 1959, aged 64.

Bibliography

Ballard, John and Suff, Paul.*The Dictionary of Football*, Boxtree, 1999

Barrett, Norman. *Daily Telegraph Football Chronicle*, Ebury Press, 1996

Betts, Graham. *United*, Mainstream, 1998

Brassington, David; Dean, Rod and Chalk, Don. *Singers to Sky Blues*, Sporting & Leisure, 1986

Butler, Bryon. *100 Seasons of League Football*, Lennard Queen Anne Press, 1998

Collett, Mike. *The Guinness Record of the FA Cup*, Guinness, 1993

Coyle, Padraig. *Paradise Lost and Found*, Mainstream, 1999

Dunphy, Eamon. *A Strange Kind of Glory*, Heinemann, 1991

Edwards, Derrick. *Footo Facts of Manchester United 1892–3 – 1995–6*, Footo Facts, 1996

Green, Benny, compiler. *Wisden Book of Obituaries*, McDonald Queen Anne Press, 1986

Green, Geoffrey. *There's Only One United*, Hodder & Stoughton, 1978

Harding, John. *Football Wizard*, Robson, 1985

Harding, John. *For The Good of the Game*, Robson, 1991

Holland, Julian. *Spurs*, Sportsman's Book Club, 1957

Inglis, Simon. *Soccer in the Dock*, Collins Willow, 1985

Joy, Bernard. *Forward Arsenal*, Sportsman's Book Club, 1954

Joyce, Michael. *Football League Players' Records 1888 to 1939*, SoccerData, 2002

Keeling, Peter. *Masters of Old Trafford*. Robson Books, 2002

Kelly, Stephen F. *Back Page United*, S Webb & Son, 1990

Kelly, Stephen F. *Hamlyn Illustrated History of Liverpool, 1892–1996*, Hamlyn, 1996

Kelly, Stephen F. *The Anfield Encyclopaedia*, Mainstream, 1993

Kelly, Stephen F. *The Old Trafford Encyclopaedia*, Mainstream, 1993

Kurt, Richard. *Red Devils*, Prion, 1998

Lamming, Douglas. *A Scottish Internationalists' Who's Who 1872–1986*, Hutton Press, 1987

Lerman, Richard and Brown, David. *The Reds*, Mainstream, 1998

McCartney, Iain. *Old Trafford: Theatre of Dreams*, Yore Publications, 1996

Seddon, Peter J. *A Football Compendium*, The British Library, 1999

Sharpe, Graham. *Gambling On Goals*, Mainstream, 1997

Sharpe, Graham. *The Book of Bizarre Football*, Robson, 2000

Soar, Philip. *Official History of Nottingham Forest*, Polar, 1998

Somerscales, Gillian; Murrell, Deborah and Pritchard, Louise. *The Official Manchester United Illustrated Encyclopaedia*, Manchester United Books, 1998

Stead, Peter and Richards, Huw. *For Club and Country*, University of Wales Press, Cardiff, 2000

Tyler, Martin. *Cup Final Extra!*, Hamlyn, 1981

Uncredited. *The Official Manchester United Illustrated History*, Carlton Books, 2001

Uncredited. *Who's Who of Cricketers*, Hamlyn, 1984

Williams, John; Hopkins, Stephen and Long, Cathy. *Passing Rhythms*, Berg, 2001

Zahra, Charles; Muscat, Joseph; McCartney, Iain and Mellor, Keith. *Manchester United: Pictorial History and Club Record*, Temple Nostalgia Press, 1986